negatives
into
positives

A PRACTICAL GUIDE TO NLP

NEIL SHAH

This edition published in the UK
in 2018 by Icon Books Ltd,
Omnibus Business Centre,
39–41 North Road,
London N7 9DP
email: info@iconbooks.com
www.iconbooks.com

First published in the UK
in 2011 by Icon Books

Sold in the UK, Europe and Asia
by Faber & Faber Ltd,
Bloomsbury House,
74–77 Great Russell Street,
London WC1B 3DA
or their agents

Distributed in South Africa
by Jonathan Ball,
Office B4, The District,
41 Sir Lowry Road,
Woodstock 7925

Distributed in Australia and
New Zealand
by Allen & Unwin Pty Ltd,
PO Box 8500,
83 Alexander Street,
Crows Nest,
NSW 2065

Distributed in Canada
by Publishers Group Canada,
76 Stafford Street, Unit 300
Toronto,
Ontario M6J 2S1

Distributed in the USA
by Publishers Group West,
1700 Fourth Street,
Berkeley, CA 94710

ISBN: 978-178578-390-6

Typeset in Avenir by Marie Doherty

Printed and bound in Great Britain by Clays Ltd, Elcograf S.p.A.

About the author

Neil Shah exists to create a happier, healthier and more resilient world. He is the founder and Chief De-Stressing Officer at The Stress Management Society, as well as Chief Insights Officer at International Wellbeing Insights. He is a leading international expert on stress management and wellbeing. An engaging and inspiring motivational speaker and success coach, he has extensive expertise in hypnotherapy, neuro-linguistic programming and strategies to promote wellbeing. He is the author of Amazon #1 best-seller *A Practical Guide to Neurolinguistic Programming* (Icon Books) and *The 10-Step Stress Solution* (Random House).

He has a vast toolbox of resources to draw from and has created all of The Stress Management Society's regular workshops. He has qualified as a practitioner in Hypnotherapy and Counselling and Communication Skills. He is a licensed practitioner of NLP, has trained as a life coach and has qualified as a practitioner of Thought Field Therapy. He is a qualified Regression Therapist, and has become accredited as an iMindMap Licensed Instructor and Master Trainer. He is also a certified Master Train the Trainer and was voted number 28 on the list of world's Top 30 NLP Professionals for 2016.

He is a member of The BACP (British Association of Counselling and Psychotherapy), the GHR (General Hypnotherapy Register) and The NHS Register of Complementary and Alternative Healthcare Practitioners. He also runs a Train the Trainer programme to equip others to deliver courses using his unique methodology and teaching style.

He is a renowned media personality on the subject of stress and also writes regularly for newspapers and magazines including the *Guardian*, *The Times*, *Men's Health*, *Psychology's Magazine*, *HR Magazine*, *Top Sante* and the *Huffington Post*. He regularly appears on television and radio interviews and is now the BBC's featured expert on stress appearing on BBC Breakfast, BBC Five Live and others. He has also appeared on Sky News, 5 News, ITV and the Dr Oz Show.

Author's note

It's important to note that there are many frequently used stories, anecdotes and metaphors employed in NLP. Where I know the source I will be sure to reference it, but my apologies to the originators of any material if I have overlooked them here.

Contents

Integrating Your Learning

What is NLP, and How Can it Help Me?

1. Preface

Over the years I have achieved tremendous success and I have also failed miserably. I had always put this down to chance, luck, fate and destiny. I was fascinated by how incredible people get incredible results and how amazing organizations achieve amazing results. Before learning about NLP I never realized that it could be easy to achieve the same results in my own life, simply by copying or 'modelling' the strategies of others who have already attained success. **In fact, NLP helps you do exactly that**.

Today I'm happy, healthy, calm and relaxed. I successfully run four companies focused on health, well-being and success achievement. I'm quoted as one of the UK's leading experts in stress reduction and relaxation.

But it wasn't always this way. Fifteen years ago my previous company failed. I was stressed out, exhausted and depressed. I had lost millions and was ill and completely burnt out. I had lost my appetite and my sex drive. I was frustrated, lacking focus, and was struggling to keep my life together. I didn't know how to deal with it, I felt helpless. I had lost my money, my car and even a lot of people whom I considered to be my close friends. I was in the lowest place I had ever been in my life.

I tried therapy – I visited my doctor, I visited a life coach, a counsellor and even a psychic healer. I read self-help books and at one point even tried anti-depressants – nothing worked!

Then I discovered Neurolinguistic Programming (NLP), **a set of concepts and techniques to understand and change human behaviour patterns**. After attending an introductory session and reading a book on NLP, I made the decision that I needed to get back on top of my life and on top of the world, so I travelled to the Himalayas with the intention of climbing Mount Everest. It was life-changing experience – as William Blake said: 'Great things are done when men and mountains meet; This is not done by jostling in the street.' I learned much about myself and my capabilities – I had to radically shift my mindset to achieve this tremendous feat. This was my first experience with reprogramming my mind to achieve success, and I'm now committed to sharing what I discovered during this experience.

My success did not come by chance. I simply took the time to understand the route I needed to take, and now I have the roadmap to take me to success – directly and effortlessly – without having to worry about getting lost. NLP can be described as a GPS system to take you to fulfilment and achievement. When I started to study NLP I quickly realized that as long as you follow the system carefully, the conditions are correct and the same process is followed, you are guaranteed to get the same results every single time. **This book is a practical introduction to that system**.

I will start by introducing you to NLP and its basic principles, ensuring that you have a clear idea of what you want. Then you will learn *how* to learn, before we explore how you can 'win friends and influence people'. The next step is to understand yourself, as we explore how to apply what you've learned and incorporate it into your life. This book is bursting with practical exercises to ensure that you learn experientially.

I would add that even though NLP is a fantastic tool, it's simply one tool, and you can't fix a car with just one spanner. Icon's other self-help books cover areas such as Cognitive Behavioural Therapy, Emotional Intelligence and the Psychology of Success, all of which can be used in conjunction with NLP. In and of itself NLP is a useful and powerful intervention. However, when coupled with other tools and techniques it can form part of a formidable toolkit for personal success or well-being.

2. About this book

Neurolinguistic Programming has been described as a popular psychological approach to enable people to have 'better, fuller and richer lives'. Unfortunately the world of NLP has become filled with jargon, technical expressions and buzzwords that just confuse people and actually prevent them from making use of simple methodologies that can have a profound impact.

The first step is to decide what your goals are. A new job? A healthier body? A better relationship? This book will help you to unlock the power of your mind and learn how to use it for your own benefit to achieve your goals!

Inside you will find:

- How to use NLP to set and achieve dreams faster, using platinum goal-setting techniques
- How to attract opportunity with a powerful new mindset
- Failsafe ways to get 100% out of your day
- How to improve your communication and negotiation skills
- How to take control of your thoughts and feelings, your state of mind, your moods, and in turn your life
- How to change negative behaviour and beliefs easily and quickly
- How to learn approaches to ensure that you fulfil your potential

- How to accelerate your ability to learn and retain new knowledge and information
- How to face your fears and phobias and overcome them rapidly
- How to remove the unconscious limiting beliefs that hold you back from success
- How to recognize some of the key robbers of energy and vitality, and how this untapped energy is available to you in great abundance if you just learn to access it
- Why it is that most people are actually not running their own lives but are responding to the beliefs and energy that they have picked up from family, friends and peer groups.

This is a practical and fun introduction to NLP and accelerated learning techniques and is written in a style that allows you to apply what you learn in real-world situations immediately.

Please bear in mind that the most effective way to learn about NLP is to experience it yourself, so be sure to have fun with the activities and exercises throughout this book. Some of them may feel unusual or strange, as they are so different from your usual way of doing things – but please just approach all the exercises and ideas with an open mind. If you don't like them or they don't work for you, then there's no need to ever do them again. However, being open to them means that you may just find something that could radically change your life.

You are limited only by your beliefs, so change what you focus on, and thereby create the life you deserve! It's time for you to fulfil your potential!

Whatever your mind can conceive and believe,
it can achieve.

Napoleon Hill

3. What is NLP?

Neurolinguistic Programming. It's a bit of a mouthful, isn't it? What does it mean, and what can it do for you?

If you're looking at this book, you've probably already heard enough about NLP to make you curious, to make you want to know more about its potential and just why so many people are talking about it. Most of all, you might want to know how ordinary people have been using it for nearly 40 years to achieve extraordinary results.

NLP is such a wide-ranging discipline that it's difficult to encompass all its branches and applications in a short definition. However, perhaps as a start we can call it a set of techniques and guiding principles that allows us to identify, model and replicate outstanding performance in any given area – guaranteeing us outstanding results. Using NLP we can eliminate or modify our existing behaviours, if we are not satisfied with them; or internalize new, more beneficial ones.

NLP isn't about dodgy new-age mantras, it isn't about hugging trees to get in touch with your inner self, and it definitely isn't about selling you snake oil. NLP is based on sound psychological principles. NLP is not a spiritual or eso-teric approach, it's an effective and rapid form of **psycho-logical therapy**, capable of addressing the full range of challenges that we're likely to encounter in our lives, such as phobias, depression, negative habits and even learning challenges. It's a wonderful tool to improve our effectiveness personally and professionally.

While traditional clinical psychology is about describing and analysing **problems** to find out their causes, NLP, in contrast, focuses on **possibilities** and how the mind works to produce results. If NLP could be summed up in one phrase, it would be **'people work perfectly'**. Our specific thoughts, feelings and actions have produced what we are today. By changing these 'inputs' you will get different results – a different you.

NLP is an **attitude**, a sense of adventure and curiosity, a desire to learn what kinds of communication can influence ourselves and others. It's looking at life as a fascinating and rare opportunity to learn and grow.

NLP is a **methodology** based on the idea that all behaviour has a structure and a process. Those structures and processes can replicated, learned, taught and even changed.

NLP has evolved into an innovative **technology**, allowing us to organize thoughts, ideas and information in ways that allow us to achieve results that are otherwise out of reach.

NLP is the art and science of personal excellence. Art because everyone brings their own unique personality and style to what they do, and this can never be captured in words or techniques. Science because there's a method and process for discovering the patterns used by outstanding individuals in any field to achieve outstanding results.

This process is called **modelling**, and patterns, skills and techniques discovered in this way are being used increasingly in counselling, education, sport and business for more effective communication, personal development and learning.

THINK ABOUT IT — Have you ever done something so elegantly and effectively that it took your breath away? Have you ever had times when you were really delighted at what you did, and wondered how you did it?

NLP shows you how to understand and model your own successes, so that you can have many more of those moments. It's a way of discovering and unfolding your personal genius, a way of bringing out the best in yourself and others.

NLP is a practical skill that creates the results we truly want in the world, while creating value for others. It's the study of what makes the difference between excellent and average. It also leaves behind it a trail of extremely effective techniques for education and business.

Neurolinguistic Programming refers to the three most important facets in creating our human experience:

neurology, **language** and **programming**. The neurological system regulates how our bodies function, language determines how we interact and communicate with other people, and our programming determines the images and models of the world we create. NLP describes the relationship between the mind (*neuro*) and language (*linguistic*) and how they impact on our body and behaviour (*programming*).

Neuro – the nervous system through which a new experience is received through our five senses and processed.

Linguistic – the verbal and non-verbal communication systems through which neural representations are coded, ordered and given meaning.

Programming – the ability to organize our communication and neurological systems to achieve specific desired goals and results.

Where did NLP come from?
NLP originated in the mid-1970s, when Richard Bandler, a maths student at the University of California with a strong interest in computer science and psychology, working together with one of his lecturers, linguist John Grinder, began leading weekly

therapy meetings that involved copying the content and style of psychotherapist Fritz Perls, who had founded the Gestalt therapy movement. This attempt to replicate the results of another person by adopting their behaviours and methods (including the moustache, chain-smoking and German accent – which eventually were deemed unnecessary!) ultimately led to the discipline of 'modelling human excellence'.

They then went on to study Virginia Satir, who developed conjoined family therapy, and Milton Erickson, who is the father of modern clinical hypnotherapy.

One of Bandler and Grinder's early books was entitled *The Structure of Magic*, and as Arthur C. Clarke once said: 'Any sufficiently advanced technology is indistinguishable from magic.' Many people have drawn similar conclusions regarding NLP. This mind science has swept across the world over the last 35 years, and using its techniques people have freed themselves of long-standing fears and phobias in a matter of minutes, or rapidly reduced the impact of the memory of a horrible experience that may have hindered them for many years.

We are led to believe that meaningful change takes time. We have all been introduced to the philosophy of 'no pain, no gain', and when a new and contrary idea is introduced, we often find it hard to believe. NLP is the kind of practice that seems 'too good to be true', which means that it has attracted both advocates and doubters, many of the doubters being among traditional psychologists whose work derives from Sigmund Freud. Let's look at how NLP differs from traditional psychology.

4. Where does NLP fit into traditional psychology?

NLP has been described as part of the next generation of psychology. However, it has not yet been accepted by mainstream academia, and is not seriously studied as a branch of psychiatry or psychology.

REMEMBER THIS!!! Traditional **Freudian psychology** and psycho-therapy requires a large commitment of time as the client tries to uncover unconscious pro-cesses that determine conscious behaviour, sometimes hav-ing to go back to relive painful or traumatic experiences.

Counselling is a shorter process, usually undirected by the counsellor, who helps the client to explore feelings and behaviour around a specific issue such as bereavement.

Cognitive Behavioural Therapy (CBT) is task-centred work that identifies a problem behaviour and how the mind thinks about it and therefore behaves in regard to it. CBT lit-erally refers to how thoughts/mental processes (**cognition**) affect behaviour. CBT then aims to alter those beliefs and thought processes, so influencing the behaviour towards a positive state for the client.

NLP has its roots in the field of behavioural sci-ence, developed by Ivan Pavlov, B.F. Skinner and Edward Thorndike. It uses **physiology** (physical and biological states) and the **unconscious mind** to change thought processes and therefore behaviour.

How is NLP different from psychotherapy?

NLP is based on 'modelling' rather than 'theory'. A model is a description of how something works, without any commitment regarding why it might be that way. NLP and psychotherapy have different underlying assumptions about the human mind and its connections with the body as a whole. NLP and traditional psychology have different methodologies, different measures and different concepts in practice. Major differences include:

• NLP is not a model of psychopathology (study of mental illness). NLP makes no diagnoses about a person's mental health or illness. Its focus is purely on results. **It proposes that people are not broken – they work perfectly to produce the results they are getting even if the results are not desirable.** If a person doesn't like the results they are getting, NLP provides tools to help them get the results they desire.

• Traditional psychology and psychotherapy patients complain that their sessions lack structure: they go in, let their thoughts wander for 50 minutes, and leave without any sense of progress; then they repeat this ritual for an indeterminate amount of time, sometimes ten years or more. Often, after years of psychotherapy, psychoanalysis or psycho-pharmaceutical treatment, while problems may have been explored and brought to conscious awareness, and even treated to reduce their effects, a person is still left with ongoing patterns that resulted from a particular situation or experience. Resolution is often left unfinished. This is not to say that traditional psychological models are useless or unhelpful. Many people have been greatly helped by them, and I would encourage anyone to explore them if that is their interest. But there's so much more that can be accomplished in far less time. For those who have already invested in psychotherapy for a number of years, NLP can be an important finishing or resolution process when psychotherapy has concluded or reached a point of diminishing returns.

- NLP is non-exclusive. In NLP we encourage people to make the most of any resource they wish to use. NLP works well either as a primary or complementary means of self-exploration and change. It doesn't take an adversarial position to psychotherapy, traditional medicine, or other alternative approaches, and clients are free to pursue any and all other avenues while exploring NLP. Some psychotherapists are equally non-exclusive and work well in cooperation with NLP coaches and therapists.

NLP and the parts model

Traditional psychology divides the mind into three essential parts: the **id**, the **ego** and the **superego**. While not all branches of psychology 'buy' this tripartite model, it remains the central and most widely used model in psychological literature and practice.

NLP also has a 'parts model', but it's metaphorical, positive and extensible. NLP proposes that internal 'parts' should be understood and used *metaphorically* rather than as literal *fact*.

The NLP parts model

In the NLP model, each of us has a non-predefined multitude of identity 'parts', some prominent at one time, others prominent at other times, all interacting with each other in some way – even if that interaction is characterized by silence or opposition.

Most of us have heard the expression, 'Part of me wants to do this, and part of me wants to do that.' In NLP this is called '**parts incongruity**'.

No part of us is considered dark or evil in NLP. Every part has a positive intention and a useful purpose, even if it's presently trying to fulfil its intention in a problematic way. Additionally, new parts can be created as needed and old parts can be changed or merged with ease.

Parts can form teams, and teams of parts can move through any number of processes for a given goal or purpose such as emotional support, creativity, healing, reality-checking, planning, critiquing, approving, action, etc.

Other features of NLP

- NLP is non-Aristotelian. This means that NLP is process- and structure-oriented, not classification-oriented. NLP proposes that putting people into categories of personality type or psychopathology promotes their getting or staying stuck, rather than assisting them to grow, change and heal.

- NLP is post-Newtonian. This means that NLP is firmly based on late 20th-century advances in physics, which observe that the universe is made up not of a collection of objects or things but of *patterns* and *processes*.

- NLP is not reductionist. NLP considers reductionism – such as the belief that our thoughts, feelings and experiences are 'just' the result of genetics or chemical processes in the brain – to be the result of linguistic confusion.

- NLP is not objectivist. NLP doesn't recognize 19th-century objectivism (a belief in absolute objective reality or the belief that 'subjective' equates to 'invalid').

- NLP is not linear. NLP doesn't limit itself to linear cause–effect thinking. It prefers whole systems thinking. Whole systems tend to be self-organizing and too complex for useful linear, cause–effect analysis.

- NLP is efficient. NLP doesn't pursue unresolvable cause–effect, question–answer sequences such as, 'Why? … Because … Why? … Because … Why? … Because …' ad infinitum, since for every answer to 'Why?', the question 'Why?' can be applied again. There is literally no end to such cause–effect sequences, and thus no satisfying resolution. With a few very specific exceptions, NLP prefers to ask more useful questions such as, 'How? What? When? Where? Who?' NLP considers that taking long personal histories from clients for causal analysis is essentially an expensive waste of time. NLP does work with personal history when appropriate – directly, as it's presently coded in a person's mind. NLP has powerful tools that a person can use to make positive changes in their ongoing experience of personal history and its meaning, patterns developed as a result of life experiences, and other factors connected with their past – without drugs, hypnosis, or years of analysis.

- NLP is not statistics-based. NLP observes that statistics cannot measure or predict a particular person's subjective experience, since subjective experience is understood by internal, not external sensory experience. NLP is the first science based on internal sensory experience.

- NLP does not share the same definition of 'behaviour' with psychology. As Bandler and Grinder pointed out in 1980, 'NLP includes within its descriptive vocabulary terms which are not directly observable.' In other words:

18

'Just because they can't see it, that doesn't mean you're not doing it or experiencing it.' And: 'Just because they can't reproduce it, that doesn't mean it didn't work for you.' In NLP, behaviours include thought structures like beliefs and values, patterns and sequences of cognition, memory, sensory representations, linguistic structures in thinking, etc., none of which can be directly observed externally, nor can their effects be directly, causally connected with measurable external observations. Yet no reasonable person would deny the importance and meaning of such internal experiences.

 For a practical example of the NLP process, and how words can change your focus and in turn change how you feel, try the following exercise. Be aware of how you feel after you finish.

Imagine you're on a beautiful beach on a lovely warm day. The skies are blue with a few wisps of cloud, the sun is shining brightly. Feel the sand between your toes as the sun warms your skin. Notice the brilliant white sand and the turquoise ocean. Hear the waves gently lapping on the shore and the breeze gently rustling the leaves on the palm trees. Smell the fresh scent of pineapples wafting over from the nearby fruit stand. Go over and choose a pineapple from the bucket of icy water they are standing in. Look at it closely, its prickly skin and its green crown. Notice how it feels cool and heavy in your hand. Press it gently with your thumb to feel how ripe and juicy it is. Lift it to your nose and be aware of its aroma. Take a knife and cut a wedge. Be aware of the sound it makes as you slice into the flesh. Notice the juices flowing from the sweet, aromatic fruit as the smell becomes stronger. Lift it to your mouth and take a nice deep bite into your wedge of golden, juicy pineapple. The sweet juices create a party in your mouth and everyone is invited. A dribble of juice drips down your chin.

It's important to remember that the above exercise is just a collection of words. A number of the words would have triggered mental, emotional and physical responses. The common assumption is that words are just describing meanings. But the truth is that they are **creating your reality**. Many of you would have felt warm, relaxed and may even have been salivating during the above exercise. This experience was created by words (language) impacting on your mental focus and nervous system (new experience impacting on the five senses) which gives you a new sensory experience (new programming).

5. Basic assumptions of NLP

Below are the eleven basic principles that underpin NLP:

1. **There is a structure to experience.** We all have patterns or structures to the way we think. The ability to change the *process* by which we experience reality can be more valuable than changing the *content* of our experience of reality.

 For example, if you like strawberry cheesecake, understand the process that you go through to get to the outcome of pleasure. Use that process on a food that you don't enjoy so much, such as spinach, and you may find that all of a sudden you enjoy spinach more than you usually do. By changing the structures, patterns and processes of the way we think, we literally change our experience, which will also have an impact on how we think about past events.

---

2. **The meaning of your communication is the response you get.** People constantly receive information that is then filtered through their internal mental map of the world. How you communicate must be constantly adjusted so the message you give is the one that is received.

3. **All distinctions that we are able to make** regarding our environment, experiences and behaviour are represented through our five senses (seeing, hearing, feeling, smelling and tasting).

4. **We have everything we need on board already** – all that we need to create change is already within us. From our vast database of thoughts, feelings, memories and sensations we can construct new mental patterns to allow us to achieve our goals and dreams.

5. **The map is not the territory.** As human beings, we can never know reality. We will only ever know our *perceptions of reality*.

THINK ABOUT IT

We don't respond to the world as it is, we act in accordance with our own mental map of the world. We experience and respond to the world around us primarily through the perceptions created by our five senses. It's our 'neurolinguistic' maps of reality that determine how we behave and that give those behaviours meaning, not reality itself. It's generally not reality that limits us or empowers us, but rather our map of reality.

We have a much better chance of getting what we want if our map is continually updated to take into account the changing territory. This is a much better approach than attempting to change the world to fit your map!

---

6. **Behind every action and behaviour there is a positive intention.** Depression could result from a need for attention. Self-harm could be using physical pain to mask the mental or emotional distress a person is experiencing. Violent behaviour could hide a lack of acceptance, or fear. Look behind how people act and what they do to find their positive intent.

7. **Our mind and body are different parts of the same system.** Thoughts, ideas, feelings and processes that take place within us and between us, others and our environment are completely interconnected. What affects one aspect of us will have an impact on another.

 Our health affects our mindset. Our mindset affects our wealth. Human negligence has led to environmental issues and climate change. Our thoughts constantly affect our breathing, muscles, immune system, heart, etc., which return the favour by impacting on our thinking. Our bodies, our communities, even our universe form a complex interdependent system, all parts of which interact with and mutually influence each other. It's not possible to completely isolate any part of the system from the rest. All systems in nature naturally seek balance or homeostasis. Control your thoughts, then you can control your mind, which in turn allows you to control your body.

---

8. **Successful communicators accept and make use of all communication/behaviour that is available to them.** We cannot not communicate. Everything about you – eye movements, body language, the tone, volume and pitch of your voice, your habits and behaviours – are all forms of communication. This is why sometimes we get a gut feeling when someone is lying to us.

 A friend was once telling me how much he cared about his mother, yet he was unaware that as he was telling me this he was shaking his head from side to side. His words were telling me one thing and his body another. This is why it's easy to get a sense of when a person is telling you something that doesn't match with who they are.

---

9. **All results and behaviours are achievements, whether they are desired outcomes or not.** If what you're doing isn't working for you, do something different. Albert Einstein described insanity as 'doing the same thing over and over again and expecting different results'. If you're not getting the results you want, do anything else other than what you're currently doing. If you do what you have always done, you will get what you always got. Do something different, anything at all, and you will get a different result.

10. **If someone can do something, anyone else can also learn to do it.** When Roger Bannister ran a mile in less than four minutes in 1954 he was the first person to break this milestone in recorded history. Since then thousands of people have achieved this feat – in fact, his record stood for only a few weeks. If we model the thinking, behaviour and actions of people who have already succeeded in a given area, we can achieve similar results.

11. **We always make the best choices available to us.** These choices are based on our experiences. More and better experiences allow for more choices. If you have had only one relationship and it ended painfully, when you meet someone new you may subconsciously associate a relationship with pain. You may sabotage that potential relationship to avoid pain. As you have more relationships and begin to associate them with fun, love and joy, you are then likely to make different, more positive choices.

All of the models and techniques of NLP are based on the above principles. According to NLP, it's not possible for human beings to know objective reality. Wisdom, ethics and a balanced ecology do not come from having the one 'right' or 'correct' map of the world, because it's not possible for us to make one. Rather, the goal is to create the richest map possible that respects the interconnected nature of ourselves and the world we live in. The people who are most effective are the ones who have a map of the world that allows them to perceive the greatest number of available choices and perspectives. NLP is a way of enriching the choices that you have and perceive as available in the world around you. **Excellence comes from having many choices. Wisdom comes from having multiple perspectives.**

Beginning to put NLP into practice

Based on my experience of NLP (and life in general) I would also include the following ideas. See if they resonate with your own life. (There will be more practical activities in following chapters.)

- **We have a natural tendency to move away from pain and towards pleasure.** If you put your finger in a flame and it hurts, you pull it away. Equally, if you want to get fit and lose weight and you happen to associate exercise with pain, you're unlikely to be highly motivated to commit to a regular routine.

 If you focus on the pleasure of the outcome rather than the activities that you associate with pain, you're much more likely to commit to regular action to achieve that goal. Don't think about 'giving up smoking' (pain) – focus on 'gaining health and well-being, energy and vitality' (pleasure). The gain will outweigh the loss.

The brain doesn't have the capacity to think in the negative. 'Don't think of a RED TRUCK' – what are you thinking about now? Your brain processes that statement as 'RED TRUCK don't think'. If you continually tell yourself, 'I want to lose weight', your brain will focus on the word 'weight' much more than the word 'lose'. The better strategy would be to have a 'target weight' on which to focus. That way the objective is to shape the body to its potential rather than losing something. NLP teaches you to always use positive language, focusing on what you want, not what you fear.

• **Using NLP, change should be easy and natural and happen in an instant**. No matter how many times you try, it's not possible to run a PC program on a Mac if it doesn't have the specific software to convert the files. And if it can do it, you may need some supporting instructions. NLP is the supporting instructions for our much more sophisticated and complex brains. It uses the brain's own language to alter and create new connections to 'convert the files' in our brains. Willpower alone is a flawed and difficult strategy. Using NLP ensures that you don't need to rely on willpower. When you know how, change becomes easy.

• **Life is not black or white**. NLP gets you away from thinking in an 'either/or' way. In NLP there's a saying: 'If you only have one way of doing something, you're a robot. If you have two ways of doing something, you have a dilemma. You need at least three ways of doing something before you have the beginnings of some real flexibility.'

One of the most basic ideas in NLP is that we change our minds not simply by having new thoughts, but by **changing the way that we think**, i.e. by choosing different ways to process the multitude of images, feelings and memories that exist inside us, so that they serve us rather than sabotage us.

 We can diminish a bad memory quite easily by giving it new associations. For example, hear a happy song in your mind every time you remember it, hear the sound of laughter, or turn the memory into an old silent black-and-white film, and see yourself happy and smiling in the image. Once you begin to associate new feelings with the old memory, how you feel about that experience changes instantly and forever. Every time you come back to that memory, you will find the new association still firmly in place.

We all have a little voice

Our little voice can be very powerful and sometimes very loud! It links in with our unconscious mind and can provide important messages and answers to problems.

Acknowledge what your little voice is saying and then ask yourself:

- Is this a helpful thought?
- What would be a more positive thought?
- Does my little voice have a warning/message I need to be aware of?
- Is there a positive reason/intention behind the message from my inner voice?

Every thought in your mind is passed via neurotransmitters around the body, linking mind and body together. How you feel physically and emotionally affects your performance. Being aware of your inner voice and thoughts can provide the answers to issues or challenges and help you respond more resourcefully and positively.

For many of us, our inner voice spends a lot of time sabotaging us and holding us back. This is a protection mechanism. It doesn't want you to get hurt, fail or experience pain, so it talks you out of things that could lead to a negative result. But we can turn our little voices into our best allies, our partners in success. Whenever your little voice isn't serving you, you can turn down the volume, or change the pitch and the tone. Imagine the little voice telling you that you're not good enough, that you're going to fail. Now give it a comical Donald Duck quack or a sexy Barry White rumble. It won't hold the same power over you when you've done this. Also, remember it's *your* voice and *you* control it. You can change what it's saying. Such methods put you in control of your reactions and thoughts.

REMEMBER THIS!!! You can learn the ability to be confident in an instant, to be more loving, or to 'make real' your ambitions before they are acted out in the world. Many successful people use NLP strategies and techniques without even knowing it, in the way they see, hear, feel, touch, and taste success in their minds long before it actually happens. The feeling of winning draws the win to it. **Visualizing a compelling future draws you towards the action needed to realize it.** In NLP, we believe that 'not all dreamers are achievers, but all achievers are dreamers'.

A method of psychology that sees the mind and body as a machine and open to manipulation is appropriate and relevant for the technology-driven culture that we live in, yet the overall effect of NLP is to increase the intensity and quality of life. **Despite its origins in computing and linguistics, NLP is really about graceful human change.**

Each of us is a bundle of emotions, behaviours and potential, all of which we must accept and even love, so as to achieve what in NLP is known as **congruence**, the perfect alignment of our desires and values with our capabilities.

Using NLP to Win Friends and Influence People

6. Communication

Communication involves a minimum of two people **interacting** with each other. People interact through a variety of channels and in many different ways – face-to-face, on the phone, through dancing, emails, letters, touch, and so on.

To become a more effective influencer – a person who can win over people much more of the time – you must develop the skill of paying very close, conscious attention to the person or people you're trying to connect with. There may be many things that you aren't currently noticing. NLP helps you to be aware that there are a whole range of things to notice in others, including:

- Language
- Eye movements
- Physiology.

The next chapter will show in greater detail how NLP can actually help us communicate more effectively. But to begin with, let's look at the nature of communication generally.

For many of us, our primary methods of communication are technology-based: email, text messaging, Facebook, etc. These require the words that we type to convey our messages for us. But is this the most effective approach?

How much of communication is words? Tone? Body language?

Most decisions are made on the basis of **rapport** rather than technical merit. You are more likely to buy from, agree with, and support someone you can relate to than someone you can't – people like people who are like themselves.

 When people are trusting and comfortable with each other, barriers come down and interesting things happen. They begin to stand, sit, move or sound like each other. They take on each other's posture, movements or voice expressions, and breathing patterns. If one moves, the other may soon follow.

How many times have you been amazed at how communication can go badly wrong, how easy it is for the slightest gesture or tone of voice to be taken the wrong way?

What is the **difference that makes the difference** in feeling comfortable and acknowledged by someone, even if they're disagreeing with what you say? How is it that some people you meet you instantly like – while others you can't get away from fast enough? Why can you talk to some people for hours and it seems like only minutes?

The answer to all of these questions is rapport – the most important process in any communication. Rapport is the ability to enter someone else's world, to make them feel that you understand them, that you have a strong common bond. Rapport is the ability to see each other's point of view (not necessarily to agree with it), to be on the same wavelength and to appreciate each other's feelings.

When people are communicating in rapport they find it easy to be understood and believe their concerns are highly regarded by the other person. At an unconscious level, there's a comfortable feeling of: 'This person thinks like I do, I can relax.' But it's important to realize that only a small amount of what we communicate is through what we say. Research has shown that in the understanding of a received communication:

- 7% is contained in the words used
- 38% is contained in the tone and style of voice
- 55% is contained in the physiology (or body language) of the deliverer.

Yet how many people actually study the factors that control over half of their communication? This is the difference between those who excel and those who just get by in the way they communicate, motivate, influence, negotiate, lead, and empower.

In particular you need to focus on the desired outcome or purpose of the communication and the extent to which this is achieved:

- What exactly do you want to achieve?
- How will you know that your communication has been successful?
- What will be the sensory evidence – what will you see, hear and feel?

We must look at what actually works. In any interpersonal communication, this means knowing where the other person is coming from – somehow bridging your different perspectives of the world.

When you're with people and talking to them, even your most positive and encouraging words will only be believed if your body language (physiology) and voice tone support your words.

With a partner, make a statement and purposefully contradict that statement with body language or tone to notice the impact on communication.

For example:

1. Tell your partner you really like what they've done with their hair while shaking your head from side to side in a negative gesture.
2. Use words to communicate to your partner that you're really angry and upset, but using a very sleepy, calm and unfocused voice tone.

Experiment with incongruence's between words, tone and body language and notice the impact it has on how the communication is received by your partner.

Frames

Any communication can be described as a set of **frames**, each dependent on the previous frames or responses.

When you make a statement, the recipient will respond in a certain way. The choice of words for your next statement will then be decided by considering this response. For example, if you present an idea while trying to persuade someone, the recipient can either accept the idea or disagree with it to varying degrees. You will need to construct your next statement by analysing this response, and choosing words so as to completely persuade the recipient.

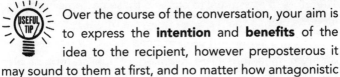 Over the course of the conversation, your aim is to express the **intention** and **benefits** of the idea to the recipient, however preposterous it may sound to them at first, and no matter how antagonistic they are in the beginning.

It's important that you always maintain a level of respect and dignity in your choice of words, so as not to offend the other person. If you come across as too aggressive or too pushy, they will most likely run away from you.

To efficiently use the persuasive patterns of language

described in NLP, the speaker must understand the finer aspects of communication, and the function of the patterns in the whole process. A **persuasion pattern** essentially comprises three parts: a frame, a response and a reframe. Once a frame is delivered by the speaker, using words to carefully describe his thoughts, the recipient will return a related response. This response will be the key to formulating the reframe statement. It's important to lead the conversation for some of the time, and let the recipient lead for the rest of it. Only then can a mutually beneficial, engrossing and persuasive conversation be held.

The method of NLP persuasion and influence isn't a one-way process: it happens in both directions. While you're trying to influence a recipient, the recipient is also trying to influence you. Therefore, it's essential to observe these patterns in an intuitive manner so that you can deliver a better response.

REMEMBER THIS!!!

A single statement used in different situations can have different meanings. The meaning of the statement also depends on other aspects such as body language, tone, facial expressions and speech delivery.

The patterns used during persuasion can be based on different NLP models, which we will cover later on in 'The Language of Success'.

The key area of rapport is covered in more detail in the next chapter.

7. Creating rapport

Harmony, accord and affinity

When you create rapport you develop a sympathetic understanding with another person. You show them that you can identify with, and even share their experience. Rapport means a relationship of **harmony**, **accord** or **affinity**.

This is the most important process in any interaction. Without rapport you will not get a productive result. The need for rapport increases in importance when you don't have it. When you do have it, many opportunities appear.

The magic of rapport is something that many people take for granted. But if you deal with people – and everybody does, unless they're a hermit living in the mountains, in which case they probably won't be reading this – the ability to create rapport between your associates and yourself is invaluable.

 The first thing you will notice when you see two people together who really get along well is *how much like each other they are*. You'll notice this most of all when you see two lovers together. They'll gaze into each other's eyes with the same expression on their faces, they'll be displaying the same body language, and they'll be speaking with the same tone of voice and pace of speech.

By observing the process by which two people get to feel more at home with each other, it's possible to enhance this effect when you're speaking to people yourself.

Most of the time we create rapport with others easily and naturally, but there are occasions when our intuitive ways of creating rapport don't work. When these occasions occur, we need to call upon certain skills to create it consciously. This is where NLP comes in. It demands focus and concentration, so that you are present in the situation rather than wishing you were somewhere else!

Rapport involves showing a genuine interest, observing how a person reacts to what you say, and identifying key words or phrases used. As we saw in the previous chapter, rapport occurs not only in what you say, but also in your actions and body language, which usually happen subconsciously.

Establishing rapport by mirroring

The process of establishing rapport needs to start with the first handshake. Creating rapport has nothing to do with liking or being liked. It's a way of saying to a person: 'We share common ground; you will be heard and appreciated.'

The key to building rapport is an ability to enter somebody else's world by assuming a similar state of mind. The first thing to realize about states of mind is that they are closely tied to body language.

THINK ABOUT IT

If someone is sitting with their arms and legs crossed and wearing a frown on their face, you can safely assume that they're not going to be very receptive to what you have to say. If, on the other hand, they have an open posture (i.e. arms and legs in fairly relaxed open positions), then they're going to be more open to what you have to say.

Have you ever noticed that when you feel depressed you tend to mope around with your head hanging, dragging your feet? Try feeling depressed while skipping and smiling – you'll find it's not possible. It's important to remember that your **emotional state** is closely tied to your **physical state**.

If you want to create rapport with someone, it's as simple as this: **you have to enter their world**. Once you enter their world you can see things from their perspective, feel the way they do, and from there enhance the whole relationship.

KEY TERM

The process by which you enter somebody else's world is called **mirroring**. The mirroring technique was created by Milton Erickson in the early 1970s in his work with clinical hypnotherapy.

Mirroring is basically copying the other person's body language, breathing and voice patterns to become like

39

them. It's literally becoming a mirror image of the other person. When you do this, you will both feel like you've known each other forever. It seems a little hard to believe at first, but once you try it, you'll see for yourself how true it is.

Some people find the idea of mirroring uncomfortable and feel that they're trying to fool or take advantage of the other person. Mirroring occurs naturally as a part of rapport-building, so don't feel you're doing anything false. All you're doing is being aware of that process and trying to enhance it. And anyway, if you feel bad about doing it, then you're probably not the type of person to take advantage of anyone anyway – so don't worry.

Start by aligning your body language. Try not to make this obvious, or it will appear that you're mocking the other person, and that will of course have the opposite effect to creating rapport. Look at things like the angle of their head, how their feet are pointing if they're standing, how their legs are crossed if they're sitting, and their facial expression. Subtly copy their posture and you will feel the whole interaction change.

 You can try half-mirroring someone if you feel uncomfortable with full mirroring at first. To half-mirror, simply do a half version of what the other person is doing. So for example, if they've crossed their arms you can hold one of your elbows with the other hand.

If they have their hands in their pockets you can put one hand in your pocket. If they're rocking back and forward on their feet, you can rock now and then. Just copy their body language to the point you feel comfortable with. The best communicators mirror without thinking.

Listen to the pace and tone of the other person's voice. If they're speaking fast, then you should speak fast too. If the person uses pauses in their sentences, then you should try to match that speech pattern. Be observant and you'll be able to pick up a lot more mannerisms than you're used to noticing – then simply copy them all. The same applies here as to the last point. If you can't make it seem natural, then perhaps ease off a little. You're trying to build rapport, not make fun of them!

Breathing is a very important part of a mental state. If you want to enter somebody else's world then you must match their breathing. This is of course closely related to speech, though it's worth mentioning as a point of its own due to the link between breathing and emotional/mental state. Observe the other person's breathing and try to match it.

 Make an effort to identify people who are in rapport. Can you see two people now who are in rapport? What do you notice about them? Is rapport something that happens actively or

41

passively? Do we get on with people because we have rapport, or do we have rapport because we get on with people? Is it a circular process, reinforcing itself?

Rapport can be tested and also reinforced by matching another person's:

- Body posture
- Voice rhythm and intonation
- Facial expression
- Common experience
- Values
- Beliefs.

Keep an eye out for people who are in rapport and notice more things that they have in common. Try it yourself. When you're talking to people, try matching different aspects from the list above. Try mismatching them too (see page 45), and notice what happens. Notice how you feel about what they're saying, and how it changes if you match or mismatch.

Mirroring or matching?

The terms 'matching' and 'mirroring' are used interchangeably by some NLP practitioners, while others draw the following distinctions:

- Mirroring is as if you were looking into a mirror. To **mirror** a person who has raised his right hand, you would raise your left hand (i.e. a mirror image).

- To **match** this same person, you would raise your right hand (i.e. doing exactly the same as the other person).

- Some practitioners also see a time difference between mirroring and matching. For example, if someone makes hand gestures while they're speaking, you would wait until it was your turn to speak before making similar (matching) hand gestures.

When should you match and when should you mirror? The only way to learn this is to practise it for real.

Matching tends to be less obvious and more outside of our conscious awareness than mirroring. Mirroring, however, tends to lead to deeper levels of unconscious rapport than matching.

Matching tonality

Tonality is something that we match rather than mirror, but it's very important that we avoid a copycat approach to vocal matching, as this will probably ruin our chances of gaining unconscious rapport. For example, a man trying to match the pitch of a woman's voice could seem ridiculous, but he could contribute towards the goal of rapport by raising his pitch within his own octave. Here are a few examples of elements of vocal tone that we can match:

- Pitch: is it high or is it low?
- Rate: is it fast or slow, steady or choppy?

- Timbre: is the voice clear, soft, croaky, raspy?
- Volume: is it loud and booming or quiet and withdrawn?

For example, if a person is speaking quickly and loudly, then you would speak quickly and loudly to match them and establish rapport. On the other hand, if the other person is speaking v-e-r-y s-l-o-w-l-y and you're talking at high speed, you're going to break the rapport.

Matching key words

Another useful technique is to match the last three or four words they say, using the same pitch, rate, timbre and volume as them.

For example, watching the football with your father-in-law, you notice that he shouts **'Go on!'** every time his team gets near the goal mouth. You, on the other hand, aren't really that interested in football, so you don't have the common frames of reference that would lead to a naturally occurring rapport state. You could, however, increase the chances of a good rapport by matching **'Go on!'** at appropriate times. Add in matching pitch, volume and tempo and you're well on your way to improving your likeability score with the old chap.

Other useful rapport techniques from NLP

Cross-matching and mismatching

If the prospect of consciously mirroring is embarrassing or daunting, you can use the concept of cross-mirroring or cross-matching. This is choosing to match one of your behaviours to a corresponding but different movement of another person. For example, if someone folds their arms, cross your legs; or pace the rhythm of someone's speaking with slight nods of your head or your breathing.

Mismatching is also a useful skill to master. Have you ever had someone go on and on and on when you were having a conversation with them? You can break eye contact, turn your body at an angle to them, breathe faster or slower ... in short, do anything to break rapport by mismatching. You'll be surprised how quickly and easily the conversation will draw to a close.

Pacing and leading

The ongoing process of mirroring or matching is known as **pacing**. You match someone's behaviour exactly, following their physiology when it changes, matching their sequence of events.

Having established rapport by pacing, you can gradually lead the person the way you want to – subtly lead them

45

into a certain voice mode, facial expression or posture with a view to changing their state of mind, while maintaining rapport, and then anything is possible.

 Pacing is frequently useful, for example when you're coaching or if you're with someone who is distressed. You use pacing to match the other person's speech, discussing the next topic only when he or she is ready to move on. It's often described as PACE, PACE, PACE and then LEAD the conversation.

If someone is extremely aggressive and talking loudly, communicating to them in a whisper isn't going to get their attention. You may need to match their tone and volume first, before slowly starting to speak more softly and calmly and thus leading them to communicating in that way.

Imagine that something has upset you. Before you're able to think rationally about it, you often need to 'get it off your chest' by talking it through with a friend or colleague. Pacing works in a similar way. You need to allow someone to say what's important to them *first*, before you start discussing *your* agenda.

Similarly, when speaking to someone, pace their speed of conversation before discussing your agenda. This may mean allowing them to discuss something that you consider

46

irrelevant but that's very important to them. Then they can pay attention and listen to what you need to say. If you interrupt people to encourage them to speak faster, you often achieve exactly the opposite effect!

Sensory acuity and calibration

As well as actively matching to increase rapport, by observing the other person for evidence of matching, you can determine the extent to which you have rapport – whether you're connecting, whether they're paying attention. This paying attention to the results of your actions is called **sensory acuity**.

At the simplest level we can deduce from a smile or a frown (or a yawn) what the other person is feeling. The most foolproof way is to first **pace** the other person and then attempt to **lead**. If they follow, you're in rapport. If not, you aren't.

Calibration is like a series of mental snapshots. The first 'shot' is your baseline against which the changes you sense will be monitored. Calibrate to verify that you're on track to your outcome and that you have willingness and agreement. Calibration keeps you out of yourself and in contact with those you are talking to, seeing the world as they see it.

The language of the senses

In the same way that you can pace and therefore lead a person's body language or voice, so you can pace and lead a person's thinking preferences and language patterns. People tell how they are processing information with the kind of words they use, the way they breathe, their tone of voice, and the way they move their eyes.

Each of us has a **thinking preference** – to 'think' in **images**, **sounds**, or **feelings**, for instance. What's more, your speech is an expression of the way you think. For example, if you think visually, you're more likely to say, 'I get the picture' or 'I see what you mean', because you do. If you think in an auditory way, you would be more likely to say, 'I hear you loud and clear' or 'We're on the same wavelength'.

The chart opposite gives clues to which sensory language to use in order to pace or lead other people.

Sensory awareness

The subtle non-verbal changes that we sense in others are a form of communication. **Sensory awareness** develops the skills to perceive these very minute differences. The tiny changes detected on the outside are indicators of what's going on inside the person. Our aim is to increase the awareness we have through our senses so that we can be in touch with the events on the inside of ourselves and others, responding accordingly. We can do this through our eyes and ears.

Thinking preferences

SEEING	HEARING	FEELING
EYES: looking up or straight ahead and defocused	EYES: looking to the side or down and left (for right-handed people)	EYES: looking down right (for right-handed people)
VOICE: high rapid	VOICE: moderate pitch, volume and rate	VOICE: low, slow, pauses
BREATHING: rapid, high, shallow	BREATHING: moderate rate, middle of the chest	BREATHING: slow, low, deep
WORDS: imagine, focus, look at, point out, seeing it, notice, show it, blind to, in a flash, review, an eyeful, picture, transparent, graphically, illustrate, brilliant, viewpoint, drawing a blank	WORDS: talk through, tune in, listen to, rings a bell, explain it, crashing down, deaf to, harmony, harsh tone, discord, an earful, outspoken, squeaky clean, calling me, hear me out, sounding off, music to my ears, keep telling myself	WORDS: hold on, put a finger on, strikes me, touched me, get a grip of, walk away, dragging me down, in touch with, out of touch with, caught in the act, underhand, touchy subject, sticking with, firm stance, no stomach for it, chilling thought

Using our sight

There are numerous non-verbal behaviours that can be seen when we know what to look for. These include:

- Speed and pace of breathing
- Lip size
- Skin colour
- Muscle change
- Body posture.

Using our hearing

Listening to voices is often made harder because we get sidetracked by the content of what's being said. Learn to pay attention to various aspects of voice quality and appreciate that any change in quality can represent a change on the inside of thinking and feeling.

- Pitch
- Tone
- Tempo
- Rhythm
- Language.

Sit with a partner back-to-back and choose an unimportant topic to talk about.

As you talk to the other person, notice the tempo and tone of his or her voice. As you talk, subtly adjust your voice until the tone and tempo of your voice are as close as possible to the other person's. Notice the quality of communication: is the flow of information smooth or difficult? Is there a feeling of rapport or not?

Try mismatching. After a few minutes of smooth, flowing conversation, alter your voice to be very different from other person's in tone and tempo. Notice what impact this change has on the quality of the communication.

Now go back to matching the other person's voice quality and notice how you're able to regain the rapport that enables a smooth flow of conversation.

THINK ABOUT IT Mirroring is a natural process to help things come into a state of harmony. Even two similar pendulums suspended with a taut wire will tend to synchronize their swinging motion. But do you always want to be in rapport with someone? Is it a good idea to choose not to be in rapport? Consider consoling someone who's depressed – do you want to get depressed too? Is that helpful to them? Would you be more or less help to them if you stayed positive?

A summary of strategies

The following list offers the key behavioural strategies that allow us to create very powerful states of rapport, both consciously and unconsciously. Mastering the art of matching and mirroring will develop your ability (and give you choices) to establish rapport with anybody you choose.

Whole body matching
Adjust your body to approximate the other person's postural shifts.

Body part matching
Pace any consistent or stylistic use of body movements; for example, blinking eyes.

Half-body matching
Match either the top or bottom of the other person's body; for example, leg movement, upper body gestures.

Head/shoulders angle patterns
Match the angles and poses at which the other person holds their head and shoulders.

Vocal qualities
Match shifts in volume, tone, pitch, pace and timbre.

Verbal
Match language patterns, styles, words and phrases used by the other person.

Facial expressions
See the ways in which the other person uses their face; e.g. wrinkles their nose, puckers their lips, raises their eyebrows.

Gestures
Match the other person's gestures in ways that are elegant and respectful.

Repetitive phrasing
Hear and use the repeated phrases of the other person.

Breathing
Adjust your breathing pattern to match another person's breathing pattern.

Indirect matching (cross-mirroring)
Use one aspect of your behaviour to match a different aspect of the other person's behaviour, e.g. adjust the tempo of your voice to match the other person's rate of breathing; pace the other person's eye blinks with your finger or head nods.

 Try the following exercise in a group of three, choosing who will be person A, B or C:

- Person A speaks for one minute about something they have really enjoyed, e.g. a holiday, party or hobby.
- Person B listens and initially matches person A in body gestures and positions. Then person B does the opposite (i.e. mismatches body language) while person A tries to keep speaking. Person B then reverts to copying person A's body language, movements and position.
- Person C observes the situation.

After the exercise, swap roles A and B so that each person tries each role. Allow person C to explain what they noticed while acting as the observer. Person A often finds it very difficult to keep speaking while person B is mismatching body language.

Four of the major NLP assumptions mentioned in Chapter 5 are particularly relevant to effective rapport:

1. The map is not the territory

We each perceive the world uniquely, as though in possession of an individual map of the world, one we have charted ourselves. These maps are made of our collection of past experiences, attitudes and beliefs. We tend to filter experience to fit our perceptions and beliefs. True communication, therefore, must attempt to understand other people's perceptual maps. By sharing other maps and adjusting our own from time to time, rapport increases and communication is made more effective.

2. The meaning of your communication is the response you get

The purpose of communication, like any behaviour, is to bring about a desired outcome, such as to pass on information, to delegate, lead, encourage, influence, or whatever. Unless it fulfils the desired outcome, it is ineffective. If the other person doesn't understand your communication, it's probably because you haven't put it in terms of their map of the world.

3. You cannot not communicate
We are all communicating all the time, mostly non-verbally. Even our inner thoughts – in effect our internal communications – are often passed on to others through our posture, body movements, facial expressions, breathing, gestures, voice tone or eye movements.

4. The mind and body are part of the same system
Our thoughts instantly affect our physiology, and this in turn affects our thoughts. When something happens outside of us (external event), we take in information through our five senses. We reduce that information by filtering it through our life's experiences. We delete, distort and generalize, and pass the information through our filters: language, memories, decisions, perceptions, values, beliefs and attitudes. That creates an internal representation of the event – the pictures in your head and the way you might talk to yourself. This in turn affects your emotional state – how you feel about it. If you have a good picture you feel great, if you have a bad picture you feel lousy. Those two affect your physiology – thinking, feeling, stance, breathing. Your internal representation, state and physiology become the driving force for your behaviour. Your behaviour becomes the input into the other person.

The Language of Success

8. NLP and language

The language that we use has an impact on the way we think, the way we act and the way we feel, and in turn the way we think, act and feel has an impact on the language that we use. Our words also have an effect on others, as theirs do on us.

Our language defines us from all other inhabitants of planet Earth. We can't even think without language, at least not in a conscious way. When you experience something enjoyable, you say to yourself, 'That was amazing'. Or you think of a problem or a challenge and you wonder, 'Why did this happen to me?', or 'How do I get through this?' Those thoughts clearly occur using language.

Language is therefore an integral part of the process of thought, as well as the way that we interact and communicate with others.

 Language is much more than a means of communication – it's also the raw material of thought.

How we communicate through language is a key area of NLP. What you say and how you say it affects other people and can influence or persuade them in different ways. You need to listen very clearly to what is being said, to notice the style of phrases and words used by other people.

Style of language often occurs unconsciously, and communication can be enhanced when people use similar styles. Language patterns, known in NLP as **meta programs**, develop throughout your life. Different life experiences will often change how you use these patterns.

Through the words used, language patterns indicate how people perceive and interpret situations. For example, some people just like to hear the 'big picture', whereas others prefer to know all the minute details – these are known as 'big chunk' and 'small chunk' styles.

We all have set patterns of thought – pre-programmed ways of processing and reacting to events and experiences going on around us. These allow us to quickly come to conclusions regarding our experiences in life without having to consciously process that experience using rational thought.

THINK ABOUT IT

Have you ever been to a party and seen someone who you found extremely attractive? The reason you felt attracted to that individual had nothing to do with them and everything to do with your program. They may have had traits or qualities that you associate with attraction. It could be they reminded you of someone you were deeply in love with, or someone who is a positive role model. This is the reason why many girls are attracted to guys that remind them of their father.

The negative aspect is that we may find ourselves constantly being attracted to partners who cheat on us or are unwilling to commit, as every new partner is selected using the same program as for the previous unsuitable partner.

Let's now look at meta programs in detail, and find out how you can communicate with people more effectively by understanding them.

9. Meta programs

Meta programs are filters through which we perceive the world. When we know which meta programs a person works to in a given situation, we can frame our communication accordingly.

An example of differing meta programs would be how two people might approach an argument. A person with what we call a 'moving away from' strategy would be likely to find any way to get away from the conflict. Someone using a 'moving towards' strategy would be more likely to head towards a specific goal, perhaps of finding an amicable solution to the conflict. The primary difference between the two is that when you're moving away from something, you never know what you may back into.

 Meta programs are unconscious filters that people develop to allow themselves to handle and respond to the high level of information and stimuli that they receive every moment of every day. After all, human beings aren't computers, thankfully. You can't process every piece of information that comes at you.

When you change these filters, it can dramatically change how you approach situations and how you perceive the world.

Meta programs are patterns of motivation and working. They drive where you put your attention, what you respond to, and what motivates you. They shape how you interact with the people and environment around you. They are your preferred way of thinking and operating. These patterns run behind the scenes, just like computer software – so automatic that you most likely don't realize they are there.

In order to appreciate the role of meta programs it's essential that we understand the relationship between **perceptions**, **thoughts** and **emotions**. For example, if our perceptions shape our emotions, what shapes our perceptions? The latest research suggests that they are filtered and re-evaluated according to our previous experiences, beliefs, values and knowledge.

REMEMBER THIS!!!

A history of meta programs

Meta programs were identified by early NLP developers as some of the habitual patterns of thinking that control how you like to work and what motivates you.

In 1957, the renowned linguist, political activist and philosopher Noam Chomsky proposed that people create their own model of the world by filtering their experiences in three different ways:

- **Deletion**: Selectively paying attention to certain information experienced through the senses, yet excluding other information.

- **Distortion**: Altering information that you receive to fit in with your beliefs or preconceived ideas.
- **Generalization**: Placing an experience in a category or group. For example, saying, 'I never win anything in the National Lottery' after buying tickets for a few weeks.

Leslie Cameron-Bandler further developed Chomsky's work in the 1970s to define particular types of deletions, distortions, and generalizations, which appear in how a person behaves. She identified a number of additional patterns. These became known as meta programs.

Subsequently, Rodger Bailey, a student of Cameron-Bandler's, further categorized these meta programs into:

- **Motivation traits**, which are the patterns that drive people to act.
- **Working traits**, which are the preferences in internal mental processing that people use in particular situations.

The ability to understand our own preferences and other people's can help in building rapport and in communicating more effectively. People with similar language patterns often show similar patterns of behaviour. For meta programs to be effective, you have to use words and phrases appropriate for the other person – saying the **right thing**, in the **right way** at the **right time**.

Pinpoint which meta program another person usually adopts, and phrase your communication using the same one. This can help the person hear and understand what you're saying faster and more effectively. For example, someone who uses a 'moving away from' meta program will respond better to a request to get on with their work if you say, 'Because you won't have to stay late', than if you say, 'Because you can go home early'.

Here are some examples of the numerous meta programs:

- General/specific (also known as big chunk/small chunk or detail/global)
- Proactive/reactive
- Moving towards/away from
- Options/procedures
- Internal frame of reference/external frame of reference
- Time orientation: In time/through time.

The following sections cover each of these meta programs in detail, including ways to identify specific patterns and recommended language to communicate more effectively with each pattern.

General/specific pattern

The general/specific meta program pattern determines how people operate at their best, based on what is, for them, the right amount of information. It defines what scope of information they work with more effectively in terms of understanding and communicating – general or specific.

Some people feel at home when dealing with details and others prefer the big picture. I'm well known among my friends for not reading instructions and avoiding detail like the plague. When I'm asked to proofread a document I often miss small errors. I love abstract conversations about concepts and I generally tend to think holistically.

By contrast, I'm lucky that my business partner Kit gets great satisfaction from obtaining every tiny piece of information he can lay his hands on. Being an accountant, he enjoys 'number-crunching' and checking that written work is entirely accurate.

Understanding general and specific patterns

Someone running the general program is likely to work well with an overview of a situation. Someone with the specific pattern requires much more information and detail. Most people start from one and move to the other. So if they start with the big picture they 'chunk down' to the detail.

In NLP the idea of chunking up or down is used extensively. Questions are asked to elicit the next level of information and bring about a new way of perceiving a situation. For instance, to 'chunk up', a useful question to ask might be: 'What is that an example of?' To 'chunk down', ask: 'What would be an example of this?'

One of the best ways to identify someone with a general pattern is to bombard them with lots of detail. They'll soon let you know because it usually drives them crazy. They love abstract concepts and have difficulty following a sequence step by step because they tend to process things all in one go. They don't tend to offer much small chunk information and can sometimes miss out important details.

People with a specific pattern love detail. They feel satisfied when they have successfully dotted all the 'i's and crossed the 't's. As the saying goes, they sometimes don't see the wood for the trees. Like the procedures pattern (see page 77), they deal with things step by step. The difference is that with a procedure there are points where another route can be taken. If you interrupt someone with a specific pattern when they're telling you something, they usually need to start from the beginning again. This is because they follow a sequence, which, unlike the procedures pattern, they don't deviate from.

Communicating with people who have a general or specific pattern

People with a general pattern prefer it when you keep the detail to a minimum. They like an overview of what you want to convey. They move conversations onto different topics in preference to discussing details.

When you're communicating with someone with a specific pattern, it helps if you use words such as 'precisely' or 'exactly'. Present information in a linear, step-by-step way. These conversations are likely to be long and drawn-out to cover all the details.

To influence people more effectively, use approaches that have meaning for their general/specific pattern:

- *For 'general' people:*
  Words: in summary, the overview, essentially, the main concept, the important thing is, the big picture, in brief.
  Style: overview, big picture, random order, generalities.
  Advantages: can make a good strategist or concept creator; can generate big ideas.
  Disadvantages: may appear to have their head in the clouds; may feel uncomfortable holding a detailed conversation; frustration with details can result in too many ideas and little execution.

- *For 'specific' people:*

  Words: exactly, in detail, specifically, precisely, step-by-step, on plan, firstly … secondly.

  Style: details, sequences, exactness, precision, specifics.

  Advantages: very comfortable working with details and excellent at spotting small mistakes; cope very well with large documents and small print.

  Disadvantages: can get bogged down in detail and work away happily, even though the purpose may have changed; may be perceived as pedantic or fastidious.

Adapting your own preference for amount and scope of information to another's has strong impact. Give less or more detail than you usually would if that's what someone else needs. In that way you experience more success in persuading, training, or instructing someone to do something.

Identifying the general/specific pattern in the context of an email is usually easy and invaluable. To influence someone effectively by email, notice how much detail goes into their own emails. You're sure to find extremes, from three words to three pages. So match the other person's style. If you want someone to approve something and their emails are very short, keep yours short too, and detail-free – just offer a concept or outline. If someone sends a detailed email to you requesting information, respond with lots of specifics.

Proactive/reactive pattern

People who operate in proactive mode are the ultimate self-motivators, the people who are regularly one step ahead. On the downside they will often ignore the analysis and planning that are needed when making important decisions. These are the leaders and drivers – the ones who are most likely to take initiative and get things started.

At the other end of the spectrum you will find people who feel more comfortable in reactive mode. They are often noted for their love of collecting information and careful planning before doing anything at all. In proactive mode, collecting information is done as part of an overall planning process; in reactive mode it's more likely to be used as a delaying tactic because they would really rather do nothing at all. That is to say, to avoid commitment and responsibility, *not* because they are lazy. These are the analysts and researchers – they may let others take the lead while they wait and evaluate the best course of action.

In proactive mode, people need very little motivation, though they can be turned off if they perceive that their initiatives are being rejected or unduly criticized. Reactive mode is better suited to group situations, where people have very little individual responsibility, and where they have a clear idea of what they are required to do and why.

It's important to note that the proactive mode really isn't the best choice in every situation. Although the business world is awash with entre-preneur types demanding that everyone be proactive, a whole team of people in proactive mode is no team at all – just a collection of individuals doing their own thing with minimum consultation, if any.

To pick up whether someone leans to a proactive or reac-tive meta program, listen to the structure and style of their communication. You will find that some are very proactive or reactive, and the rest a mix of the two.

When watching the news, try to identify indi-viduals who are proactive and reactive using the following characteristics:

Proactive language
Short, sharp sentences
Direct
Active verbs
Engaging
Passionate
Fast speaking

Proactive body language
Very animated
Lots of hand gestures and gesticulation
Fidgeting

Focused
Eye contact

Reactive language
Long, drawn-out sentences
Failure to get to the point
Passive verbs
Incomplete sentences
Words such as 'but', 'should', 'would', 'could', 'might'
Monotone

Reactive body language
Little or no eye contact
Ability to sit still
Little animation and limited use of hand gestures and
  gesticulation
Calm

Using the proactive/reactive program

Use specific strategies to influence people based on whether they identify with the proactive or reactive meta program:

- *For proactive people:*
  Words: go for it, let's do it, get the job done, now, don't wait, take control, make things happen (words or phrases about action and doing).

Style: get things done, take control, take charge, take action; enjoy taking charge, finding solutions and moving at a fast pace.

Advantages: willing to take action; assume leadership roles.

Disadvantages: can ignore analysis and planning.

- *For reactive people:*

  Words: why not think about it, consider, could, might, analyse, think about, take your time (words and phrases with choices).

  Style: wait for others to take the lead, analyse choices and goals, wait for instructions, slower pace, take time to think about things carefully.

  Advantages: good analysts and researchers; evaluate the best course of action; weigh up all the data before acting.

  Disadvantages: tendency to avoid commitment and responsibility; may procrastinate.

Moving towards/away from pattern

The moving towards/away from meta program pattern focuses on what motivates people to do something.

Generally we take action because:

- We have a desire to **move towards** something: perhaps a goal, dream or target.

- We want to **move away from** something: for example a challenge, a problem or a difficult situation.

 When asked, 'What's important to you about a car?', a 'towards' person will answer with what it can give them: speed, status, the opportunity to impress other people, etc.

An 'away from' person will respond by what a car will keep them from: 'It won't break down, it's not expensive, I don't want to spend huge amounts of money on petrol and maintenance', etc.

You'll note the same when asking, 'What's important in relationships?'

Towards: Fun, connection, love, affinity, etc.

Away from: Not an alcoholic, doesn't scream, doesn't 'play games', no drama, etc.

 What would motivate you more in each example below?

1. Your football team winning the league, or preventing them from being relegated?

2. Winning the race, or concern about not being able to finish?

3. Having financial security, or fear of being bankrupt or broke?

4. Focus on success and achievement, or fear of failure?

5. Would you work harder to achieve pleasure or avoid pain?

This will give you some insight into whether your natural tendency is to run a 'towards' program or an 'away from' program.

The 'towards' pattern
If you are motivated by a 'towards' pattern you will generally be more focused on **what you want**. You're likely to work towards objectives such as:

- Achieving a particular goal or target
- Gaining promotion at work
- Fulfilling a sporting goal
- Activities that bring you pleasure.

You will find it easier to focus on the benefits of the activity. You will find that you're energized by targets and outcomes. As you focus on what you want to accomplish, you tend to set priorities well. When operating at the extreme of this pattern, you may struggle to identify potential problems or recognize possible barriers to success. When also running a strongly proactive pattern, you may develop an almost kamikaze approach.

 A person in towards mode thinks in positive terms, identifying what they want to achieve. They have an image in their mind of what they want and they move more or less directly towards the realization of their goals. If the towards attitude is too strong, it can seem aggressive and insensitive rather than assertive.

The 'away from' pattern

If you run a strong 'away from' pattern, you're more likely to focus on **what could go wrong** in a particular situation. You're likely to work hard to avoid:

- Challenges
- Difficult situations
- Crises
- Disasters.

You're likely to be motivated by:

- Problem-solving
- Identifying actual and perceived challenges and threats
- Being aware of everything that could go wrong.

If your motivations are truly 'away from', you're likely to be easily distracted from objectives because you feel compelled to deal with any problems that arise. Any deadlines or priorities that you have agreed are likely to be forgotten as you troubleshoot the latest issue to emerge.

You will find that you're much clearer about what you're trying to avoid than about what you want to achieve, and this inability to express a positive desire can make it very hard for you to formulate any kind of outcome.

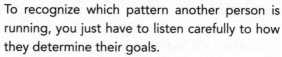

How do we know which pattern is running?

To recognize which pattern another person is running, you just have to listen carefully to how they determine their goals.

When someone says, 'I'm going to do XYZ *because* …', listen very carefully to what comes next – it will tell you whether (in that particular context) their motivation is to work towards or away from the stated result.

Do they discuss their dreams and what they want to achieve? (Towards)

Or do they tell you what they want to avoid, and all the challenges that could prevent them from fulfilling their objectives? (Away from)

For example:

1. My dream is to live in a large house in the country and be financially secure. (Towards)

2. My dream is to get out of this neighbourhood and not be unemployed. (Away from)
3. This new contract will allow us to expand our business, raise salaries and buy new equipment. (Towards)
4. This new contract will mean we don't have to make redundancies, we can avoid a crisis, and don't have to worry about old equipment failing. (Away from)

Which of these two motivation directions is better?

It's impossible to state this unequivocally because there are no 'better' and 'worse' programs. It can be assumed that a towards pattern will be more useful in many situations where we're focused on positive matters, on goals and not on obstacles. On the other hand, the ability to perceive the potential obstacles and difficulties is also a valuable one.

For **motivation** purposes, a person in 'towards' mode needs to be pointed in the right direction and be clear about the reward for achieving their goal (with occasional discreet checking to ensure that they stay on track). A person in 'away from' mode can be motivated by threats – however, be careful: if the threats become too intense, they may become afraid to do anything at all.

 In NLP there's a mantra: **'Energy flows where attention goes.'** When considering this particular meta program, it's important to bear this in mind. We tend to get what we focus on. If we focus on our problems, we get more problems and we tend to attract more challenges. When we focus on what we're grateful for and what's working well for us, we will find reasons for success and gratitude. This has been labelled the 'Law of Attraction' and has been covered in great detail in the international bestselling book and film *The Secret*.

I attribute much of my success to 'energy flows where attention goes', especially when it's paired with action, responsibility, hard work, and setting well-formed outcomes.

Using the towards/away from meta program

Use specific strategies to motivate people based on whether the 'towards' or 'away from' meta program is identified:

- *For 'towards' people:*
  Words: fulfil, gain, get, attain, accomplish, achieve, the advantages, have, obtain what you want, benefit, bonus, target, include (words or phrases that take the person towards a target).
  Style: towards the positive, goal-oriented.
  Advantages: forward-thinking; goal-oriented; positive energy and drive.
  Disadvantages: may get entangled by too many new initiatives at once; may be perceived as 'gung-ho'; have a tendency to leave things unfinished.

- *For 'away from' people:*

  Words: avoid, exclude, recognize problems, not have, prevent, fix it, avoid, steer clear of, find out what's wrong, there will be no ..., solution, remove (words or phrases that take the person away from a situation)

  Style: away from the negative, avoiding problems.

  Advantages: very good at assessing risks and recognizing what to avoid.

  Disadvantages: overly cautious with a tendency to focus on the downside; may appear negative and unwilling to try new experiences; makes choices based on avoidance rather than a desire for something new.

Options/procedures

Are you always looking for better or alternative ways to do things, or are you more likely to follow a tried-and-tested method? The options/procedures meta program is extremely useful to understand how you approach tasks and tackle challenges.

- **You're probably motivated by the options pattern** if you're motivated by choices, variety, and the chance to do something differently or better than previously. You may be very good at drawing up procedures for getting the job done, but you have no interest in following the procedure yourself. You initiate a new project with bravado but may not ever complete it. You look at all the possibilities and when you have plenty of choices you take action 'just because you can'.

- **You're probably motivated by procedures** if you believe a 'right' way to do things exists. You like your work to have a start point and an end point – basically you get things done. You can find having too many choices about how to handle things difficult. You take action when you have the comfort of clear instructions or recommendations. You're likely to take action because you feel you 'have to'.

Identifying options/procedures patterns

Someone's options or procedures preference is usually expressed in how they speak.

- Someone with the options preference uses a lot of 'I can' and 'I could'. They're more likely to recognize an opportunity and take action.
- Someone motivated by the procedures preference uses a lot more of 'I must', 'I had to', 'I had no choice' and 'I should'.

- **Options** people enjoy breaking or bending the rules. Exploring new ideas and possibilities is of great interest to them. To motivate or influence these people, use words such as: opportunity, alternatives, break the rules, flexibility, variety, unlimited possibilities, expand your choices, options.

- **Procedures** people like to follow set rules and processes. Once they understand a procedure they will repeat it over and over again. They have great difficulty developing new processes, and without a clearly defined procedure they feel lost or stuck. They're more concerned about *how* to do something than *why* they should do it. Bending or breaking rules is heresy! They're motivated by words such as: correct way, tried and true, first … then … lastly, proven path, follow this procedure to the letter.

When they're in 'options' mode, many people have a strong streak of creativity, which they may find difficult to control. They prefer to find their own route – usually with many diversions along the way!

When someone is in 'procedures' mode they find choices distracting, and given half a chance will follow a set policy to the letter, often with no regard for the consequences.

A person in options mode really doesn't need motivating, as self-motivation is one of their main strengths; rather they need to be kept firmly (but not too obviously) on track. A person in procedures mode is best motivated if they're given detailed instructions, the need to make choices is minimized, and they can earn praise when they adhere to the standard procedures.

Using the options/procedures program
Use specific approaches to influence people based on their preference for options or procedures:

* *For an options-motivated person:*
  Words: possibilities, choice, play it by ear, alternatives, options, new, break the rules, variety (words or phrases that offer options).
  Style: love variety and different possibilities, start projects but don't always finish them, willing to try new ways and offer choices.
  Advantages: explore many options and provide people with choices; happy to test and break rules.
  Disadvantages: may procrastinate and avoid making decisions until forced to do so by circumstances; very good at reinventing the wheel.

* *For a procedures-motivated person:*
  Words: the right way, tried-and-tested, first ... second ... and then ... (words or phrases with clear structure and procedure).
  Style: follow set rules, methods and procedures; like precise instructions, follow speed limits!

Advantages: very efficient; good with rule-based administration; will stick to agreed notes.
Disadvantages: the procedure may become more important than the job to be done; at worst bureaucratic and blocking.

Internal/external frame of reference

The phrase 'frame of reference' refers to where you put your attention.

When you reference **externally**, you get your sense of self from things, events, and circumstances outside of yourself. If you're externally referenced you will define yourself by your title, status, car, home, where you go on holiday, past, future, parents, children, needs, or condition. You're on a constant journey of reaffirming who you are – to yourself.

When you reference **internally**, life is much simpler. You know who you are. You know why you're here. You know what gives you your greatest sense of satisfaction. You know what you want to contribute. You know what you want to leave behind after you're gone and you're doing something about it now.

An external frame is about getting your needs met. An internal frame is about living your life fully present, fully expressing your core values.

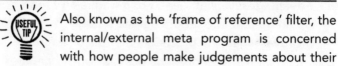 Also known as the 'frame of reference' filter, the internal/external meta program is concerned with how people make judgements about their own actions. If you ask someone, 'How do you know when you've done well at a given task?', they may answer that they go by other people's reactions (external), or that they base success on how they feel (internal) – or they may use a combination of the two.

People with a significant element of external reference are relatively easy to motivate since your approval, or disapproval, will directly affect their perception of whether they're performing well. Indeed, they can sometimes seem over-responsive, because someone in external mode will often hear other people's input, even mild suggestions or queries, as commands.

People with an internal frame of reference are really only interested in their own opinions. Where someone in external mode hears input as commands, a person in internal mode hears external input, even direct commands, as mere information. These people may be hard to motivate unless you frame your approach in the appropriate terms.

People who are chiefly internal will assess something as being 'good' through internal standards/beliefs and 'gut feelings'. They will say: 'I just know it's good', or 'It makes me feel good'.

People who are chiefly external will have a list of criteria as a reference for what is 'good', saying, 'It has this and this quality', or perhaps mentioning that other people value it.

Internal people have difficulty accepting other people's opinions and outside direction, even if they are good ideas. If they receive negative feedback on something they believe they have done well, they will question the judgement of the person giving the feedback. They may gather information from outside sources; however, they will assess it based on their own internal standards. You can motivate this type of person by the following words: you know what's best, only you can decide, it's up to you, I need your opinion.

External people need outside direction and feedback to stay motivated and to know how well they're doing. Without external validation, they may feel lost or have difficulty starting or continuing an activity. They may interpret a simple discussion as an order and then feel swamped with all you've directed them to do. They're motivated by words such as: according to the experts, others will think highly of you, you will be recognized for your efforts.

Using the internal/external frame of reference program

To motivate based on an individual's feedback pattern, use specific strategies:

- *For people with a strong internal program:*
  Words: you know, you may wish to consider, you may want to think about, only you can decide, a suggestion for you, up to you, what do you think? (words or phrases about personal feelings).
  Style: know within self, use own feelings, happy to make own decisions.
  Advantages: can stay motivated when there's little feedback or praise.
  Disadvantages: internal standards may override, and sometimes cancel out, external evidence; will disregard evidence, facts, and sound advice from other people.

- *For people with a strong external program:*
  Words: the feedback is, results show that, the person with authority says, what I've noticed, the word on the street is, opinions are, statistics show (words or phrases about other people).
  Style: depend on others, facts and figures, need feedback.
  Advantages: will make decisions based on concrete facts and evidence, or maybe just the 'feel good' factor, so long as it comes from an external source; able to give excellent customer service and help to others.
  Disadvantages: will get stressed when there's a lack of external feedback; needs frequent feedback on

performance to make good progress; will be indecisive if there's a lack of feedback.

Time orientation: In time/through time

This meta program describes how people arrange their perception of events past, present and future. This pattern can also be called inside time/outside time.

In time describes someone who becomes caught up in the stream of events in their lives. They can only 'see' events in the immediate future and the immediate past, which tend to be straight in front of them and right behind them, respectively. This makes it difficult for someone 'in time' to look objectively over past events, plan ahead, estimate the time required to complete a task – or turn up on time. But they do value each moment.

Someone in **through time** mode, however, 'sees' events as something like a stream flowing past in front of them. They're better able to view the past and plan ahead, and thus see how events are developing. They spend their time planning and making sure they're not late for meetings. However, their preoccupation with planning their next moment or analysing the last may prevent them from concentrating on the matter in hand.

Using the time orientation meta program

To motivate based on an individual's time orientation pattern, use these specific strategies:

- *In time people:*
  Words: now, here, enjoy the moment, be present, be aware of, feel, (words or phrases that are focused on the present).
  Style: live in the moment, spontaneous, impulsive, don't look back or to the future much.
  Advantages: can concentrate on tasks; emotionally and mentally engaged in each activity and every experience.
  Disadvantages: frequently late and can give the impression of not being concerned about timekeeping; may get involved in too many things through attachment.

- *Through time people:*
  Words: In the past, next time, previously, last time, in future, historically (words or phrases about the past or future).
  Style: preoccupied by thoughts of the past and future, often neglecting the present moment.
  Advantages: good planner and timekeeper.
  Disadvantages: may give the impression of not being engaged in the current activity; being on time, and scheduling activities, can become more important than the activities themselves.

10. The meta model

One of the chief benefits of NLP is to increase flexibility of response. But being able to respond to a situation using only a meta program can limit your choices and ability to enjoy life. The aim of this section is to give you greater choice in how to perceive and respond to everyday situations.

As a general rule of persuasion, you must use a person's existing meta program to persuade them of your outcome. But this process is less persuasion than an exercise in **personal development** and **flexibility**. As a further benefit, if you wish to have meaningful conversations or relationships with others who have different meta programs, you need to respect their models of the world, be flexible and speak to them in their language. Thus by applying this technique you will better understand other people's perspective on the world.

Filtering language

As we saw in Chapter 9, in conversation we unconsciously use three filters or processes: **deletion**, **distortion** and **generalization**. These filters transform what we experience with our senses into our internal thoughts. They clarify our experiences and help us to interpret the true meaning behind what people say.

They can work positively and negatively. You can identify the filter a person is using by listening to signs in their language. When you recognize the pattern being used, you can ask specific questions to ascertain the true meaning of their communication. These specific questions were originally developed by Richard Bandler and John Grinder in 1975, and are referred to in NLP as the **meta model**.

 If we recognize which filters people are using, we can anticipate how they're likely to react to what we do and say – this is where meta models are useful. With a language filter identified, questions can be phrased more specifically to gain greater understanding. Questioning helps to:

- Gather more information to find what may have been left out or **deleted**

- Clarify meaning, when evidence has been **distorted** from the true meaning

- Identify a limitation, to offer more choices when information has been **generalized**.

We communicate in words by deleting, distorting and generalizing the **deep structure** of our experience into a spoken **surface structure**. The meta model is a set of language patterns and questions that reconnect the deletions, distortions and generalizations with the experience that generated them. The meta model questions 'reverse engineer', working on the surface structure to gain insight into the deep structure behind it.

As Richard Bandler and John Grinder noted in 1975:

> *With the artful use of Meta Models, the practitioner can involve the client in recovering the deep structure – the full linguistic representation. The next step is to challenge that deep structure in such a way as to enrich it. […] The basic principle here is that people end up in pain, not because the world is not rich enough to allow them to satisfy their needs, but because their representation of the world is impoverished. Correspondingly, then, the strategy we, as practitioners, adopt is to connect the client with the world in some way that gives him a richer set of choices. In other words, since the client experiences pain by having created an impoverished representation of the world and forgetting that the representation is not the world, the practitioner will assist the client in changing just in case he comes to behave in some way inconsistent with his model and thereby enriches his model.*
>
> *The Structure of Magic*, Volume 1

KEY TERM

The name '**meta model**' came about because 'meta' means 'above' or 'beyond', so the meta model is a model of language on language, clarifying language by using language itself.

What does a meta model do?

A meta model seeks to understand the underlying perspective of the individual. When an individual is asked to describe their problems, they will usually constrain their choice of words, modify, generalize or remove certain information that was part of the actual experience. The person will usually portray the situation in close relation to their understanding of the experience, and will not usually give out all the details that caused, or occurred during, that event.

The meta model comprises a set of explicit questions and language patterns that are intended to question and enlarge the boundaries of the map of perception of that individual as regards the surrounding world. Typically, questions may be in the form of:

- 'What X, specifically?'
- 'How, specifically?'
- 'According to whom?'
- 'How do you know that?'

A way of making sense of the meta model is to be aware that not everything that is being thought of is actually put into words, resulting in deletion of certain facts or observations. Several assumptions could be made by the individual and there could be structural incorrectness compared to the facts, leading to a distortion in the event portrayed. There could also be an inclination to use wide-ranging statements leading to generalization of the core idea or problem at hand. In addition to this, the listener might not fully comprehend or correctly interpret what is being said, and the image generated after being filtered through their own set of beliefs and assumptions might drastically deviate from the actual truth.

Let's look at the three categories of the meta model and how to recognize them in everyday speech.

Generalizations

Definition: 'One example is taken to be representative in a way that narrows possibilities. The process of creating a general rule or assumption on the basis of a very limited amount of evidence.'

Think about words that raise emotions in otherwise rational people: 'You always say that.' When you spot a permanent, all-embracing word like 'always', 'never', 'every', 'all' or 'none', you're probably on to a type of generalization known in NLP as a **universal quantifier**. These words are deadly, in that they eliminate nearly all of the choices and alternatives that better thinking provides. They can end conversations and relationships and induce ulcers. The effective response is to pose the universal word as a question: 'Never?', 'Always?', etc. This usually exposes either an absurdity or at least an exaggeration. Having raised doubt about the universality or permanence of the statement, you can explore further: 'In what circumstances might you ...?', or 'Have there been occasions when [e.g.] he wasn't late?'

 Watch out also for cases where the offending words are missing but implied. 'Takeaway food is unhealthy' implies that *all* takeaway food is unhealthy and is another example of a generalization.

Start off by spotting the common words. Then, with practice, you'll begin to spot the hidden patterns.

Another common pattern includes words like 'cannot', 'possible', or 'impossible'. How often have you heard expressions like 'You can't do it like that' or 'That's impossible'? These are just as restricting, if unchallenged, as 'never' or 'always'. They are clarified by asking the question: 'What would happen if you did?', or 'What exactly is stopping you?' In doing this you'll be able to distinguish between what is *really* impossible, and what is a type of generalization called a **modal operator of possibility**. Getting what you want involves habitually attempting to achieve the impossible.

Its sister pattern, the **modal operator of necessity**, is signalled by words like 'should' and 'should not', 'must' and 'must not', 'ought' and 'ought not'. Again, you can respond: 'What would happen if you did?' A lot of these patterns date back to childhood and social conditioning. They're based on rules that may be long past their sell-by date, yet are still part of our language and thoughts. 'You shouldn't mix with those people' invites the response: 'What would happen if I did?' Challenging these codes of necessity doesn't imply rebellion or anarchy, just healthy questioning to see if choices are being unknowingly missed.

Note that this and other meta model responses don't ask 'Why?', but 'What? or 'How?' The technique explores alternatives without setting any moral agenda, aiming to create alternative points of view, and more possible outcomes.

The final generalization, known as a **complex equivalence**, is when two statements are put together as though they mean the same thing. Example: 'She must be tired … she's been running around all day', or 'He's not smiling … he's not enjoying himself'. In these cases, 'running around all day' is taken to be equivalent to 'being tired' and 'not smiling' equivalent to 'not enjoying himself'. These are more insidious than 'never' and 'can't', as there are no obvious words to watch for. The meta model response is: 'How does *this* mean *that*?'

Usually it's obvious that the statements aren't equivalent, so the skill is in spotting the pattern rather than coming up with a clever exposé of the misuse of language.

GENERALIZATION – taking specific experiences and creating a general principle

Examples of language used
'Everything is going wrong.'
'This always happens.'
'Everyone gets in the way.'

Questions to ask
'Everything or just one aspect?'
'Always or just occasionally?'
'Everyone or just someone?'

AIM: To expand the conversation away from the limits the person is setting.

HOW: Ask questions to ascertain if it happens every time and if it's always the case. Use: 'Every time?' 'What would happen next?' 'What stops you?'

Deletions

Definition: 'Important information is left out and limits thoughts and action. The process of ignoring certain items of information about some event or person (for any reason).'

Deletions are the language that's missed out before it becomes a spoken or written communication. Think of the common expression: 'It's a matter of opinion.' What is? The noun 'it' is unspecified. Or: 'They're out to get me.' Who are they? 'Things are getting out of hand.' What things?

Unspecified nouns are clarified by asking: 'Who or what specifically?'

Not only do we omit specific nouns, we do the same with verbs to equal effect. 'He lost his watch' – how did he lose it? 'She hurt her leg' – how did she hurt it? Many verbs, although they are 'doing' words, leave out lots. Words like 'travelled', 'helped' or 'worked' don't tell us *how*, so we're left guessing what exactly happened, or what was done. Unspecified verbs are clarified by asking: 'How, specifically?'

Sometimes verbs describing an ongoing process are turned into nouns. For example, the verb 'educate' becomes 'education', and 'fulfil' becomes 'fulfilment'. Such nouns seem intangible – you can't wrap education in a box or lock fulfilment in your garage. So a lot of specific meaning is lost when we use **nominalizations**, as they're called. Words like 'respect' can have very different meanings, depending, for instance, on who is respecting whom, and how that respect is demonstrated.

THINK ABOUT IT

Business and government communications are often full of nominalizations, which is why it seems that a lot of words are used when little meaning is communicated. To get at the missing information you have to turn the nominalization back into verb form, and ask **who is doing what, and how are they doing it**? Who is educating whom and how? 'She has a bad memory' (a nominalization) raises the question:

'What does she not remember [the verb], and how does it affect her?'

Distortions

Definition: 'Information is twisted in a way that limits choice and leads to unnecessary problems and pain. The process of reshaping information so that it misrepresents external reality (for any reason).'

The distortions category of language patterns includes everyday language that you will be familiar with. Have you ever had someone make a statement like: 'You're not sure, are you?' Or: 'You won't like him.' This is quite simply *mind reading*! And this sort of statement only makes sense if we can read each other's thoughts. These patterns are used when someone thinks they know, without evidence, what another person is thinking or feeling. For example: 'He was delighted, but just didn't show it.' We make these assumptions all the time, often based on non-verbal cues that we think we understand.

IF YOU REMEMBER ONE THING As with all these common language patterns, we're likely to see distortion used by others long before we recognize it in ourselves.

There's a fascinating variation on this mind-reading theme. Sometimes we wrongly assume that people *can* read minds, and language supports this: 'You knew it would upset me.' Or: 'You must have known I wouldn't like that.' 'Mind reading' and 'projected mind reading' are classic recipes for disagreements and conflict.

How do you respond to mind reading? By asking a question:

'Cathy doesn't care about me.'
'How do you know Cathy doesn't care about you?'
'Because she never calls or asks about my work anymore.'

The question has elicited another statement, which forms a **complex equivalence** (not asking about work is equivalent to not caring) and also includes the **universal quantifier** word 'never'. By asking the question 'Never?', you can put the work discussion in context. Then you can go on to ask: 'How does *this* mean *that*?', which will soon show up any false link between the two statements.

Another distortion that's closely related to the complex equivalence is the familiar pattern of **cause and effect**. 'He's been happier since she returned' assumes that 'her returning' is the cause of him 'being happy'. It's easy to miss these and fall into the trap of assuming a link when no cause and effect relationship exists. You clarify this language pattern by asking: 'How, specifically, does this cause that?'

A close relationship to the cause and effect pattern is a **presupposition**. 'Shall we meet at your place or mine?' presupposes that you're willing to meet, and if so at one of the venues mentioned. 'Would you like red or white wine, sir?' presupposes that sir would like wine. Presuppositions can be challenged by asking: 'What makes you believe that …?'

DISTORTION – changing the meaning

Examples of language used	Questions to ask
'Wearing that outfit means you don't take this job seriously.'	'What specifically about this outfit makes you think that?'

98

Examples of language used	Questions to ask
'Sitting next to Alexia at the party means she'll like you and want to date you.'	'How does sitting next to her guarantee that she'll want to date you?'
'Your comment made me upset.'	'How exactly did what I said make you feel upset?'

AIM: To ascertain the underlying meaning.

HOW: Ask questions related to how you know and what the evidence is. Use: 'Who says?' 'How do you know?'

 People respond to events based on their internal pictures, sounds and feelings. They also collect these experiences into groups or categories that are labelled with words. The meta model is a method for helping someone go from information-poor word maps back to the specific sensory experiences that they're based on.

It's here in the information-rich specific experiences that useful changes can be made that will result in changes in behaviour. This can be used to change your own behaviour as well as that of others.

---

11. Employing the language of success

How can an understanding of the meta model patterns help you to get what you want?

Most of what we do involves other people, and so-called 'successful' people seem to be good communicators. The meta model puts interpersonal communication onto another plane, and makes language work *for* you rather than *against* you. You will have seen that there's a standard type of response to every pattern. This doesn't mean that you will always have to use the response in conversation. Merely recognizing a pattern and being able to question it mentally will change the way you perceive a situation, how you feel, and how you behave.

Making it work for you

Knowing that a language pattern exposes an absurdity means that you won't let it affect you in a serious way – your feelings will be influenced by your interpretation of the statement, and your interpretation will take account of any defect in the language. So you should no longer be fooled by statements that try to limit what **you can or should do**.

Where you spot a deletion, and you want to gather more information, you're free to make a response and get better understanding, **for your own purposes**.

You need not build your own outcomes on untruths, be they presupposition, mind reading, or wrong cause and effect relationships. Nor need you be tricked into making meaningless comparisons. When you formulate your goals and plans you will instinctively avoid nominalizations and start using words that have specific, motivating **meaning for you**.

The inner voice

As we saw in Chapter 6, much of language is not physically spoken. It's that self-talk, or inner voice, the way you think things out, or express what you feel to yourself. Much of this dialogue, which is very close to the surface and so suffers from the same deficiencies as spoken language, takes on the form of meta model patterns. **So you're as likely to be deluded by your own inner voice as by other people's.**

'You can't do that' might be something you say to yourself far more than it's said to you by others – and you're far more likely to believe yourself. All the meta model responses, therefore, also apply to your inner voice. Where you need to be very careful in your tone of voice when making a response to someone else who might be antagonized, you need not be so considerate with yourself.

IF YOU REMEMBER ONE THING

Meta model skills help you to clarify your own thinking and control your own feelings, as well as helping you to express yourself and negotiate persuasively.

TRY IT NOW!

Find a feature or editorial piece in a popular newspaper or magazine and see how many meta model patterns you can spot. Go over the text a few times – each time you will probably find new examples. Then scribble down the responses you would use, imagining you were addressing the writer of the article or the people being quoted.

Next, make a point of listing meta model language patterns when at work, at home and in a social setting. See which ones are the most common. Don't try to pick up every word, just listen, identify patterns (even if you can't put them into a category), and mentally form a response.

These exercises will help you to see things in a very different way, will give you greater objectivity, and will mean that you take more control of your feelings, giving you more control of your life and what you do with it.

What can the meta model do for you?

- **Gather information:** By challenging deletions, the meta model recovers important information that has been left out of the surface structure.

- **Clarify the meaning**: It gives a systematic framework asking: 'What exactly do you mean?' When you don't understand what another person means, that is your cue to ask meta model questions.

- **Identify limits:** By challenging the rules and generalizations that you're applying to your own thinking, the meta model questions show where you're limiting yourself and how you could be freer and more creative.

- **Give choices**: By showing the limits of language and thought, especially where distortions are limiting clear thought and action, the meta model expands your map of the world. It doesn't give the right answer, or the right map, but it enriches the one you have.

12. Embedded commands

In the previous chapter we looked at the meta model pattern of presupposition, which can be used to manipulate people in situations such as politics and advertising. But what would happen if we used such techniques to influence people? Would that make us bad people? My belief is that if we're using techniques such as the ones I'm about to introduce to you with **positive intent**, to influence someone to a 'win-win' outcome, or to get the kids to bed, or help your colleague finish his project, or even get yourself upgraded on that flight, then it can't be regarded as manipulation – and definitely will not reflect negatively on you.

Embedded commands are patterns of language that bypass conscious reasoning and speak directly to the subconscious mind. Embedded commands influence people at the subconscious level. This allows you to direct people to take specific actions.

Your brain is always analysing what's going on around you. It's trying to find similar things from your past and trying to line them up with each other. The subconscious mind has stored millions of conversations with other human beings. These conversations have become so routine that the mind has virtually fallen asleep.

Your subconscious mind runs on autopilot. It's accustomed to remembering or responding to stuff day after day. Remember, the older you get, the more you think, 'autopilot has heard this before'.

When using embedded commands correctly, you create unusual patterns of language that force the subconscious mind to **wake up and pay attention**.

Well, what's the result? The subconscious has received a direct and specific command that it feels compelled to act on.

Viruses of the mind

Embedded commands are techniques for 'planting' a thought (state, process, or experience) within the mind of another person beneath the person's conscious awareness. This is done through **presuppositions**, which are assumptions implied within verbal structures, as we saw in Chapter 10. If you think of an embedded command as a 'virus of the mind', then the phrase used to deliver that command is the invisible hypodermic needle used to inject that 'mental virus' into the mind of your target. This phrase is known as a **weasel phrase**.

CASE STUDY

Weasel words or phrases are aimed at creating an impression that something specific and meaningful has been said, when in fact only a vague or ambiguous claim has been communicated. For example, an advertisement may use a weasel phrase such as: 'Up to 50% off on all products.' This is misleading because the audience is invited to imagine many items reduced by the proclaimed 50%, but the words taken literally mean only that no discount will exceed 50%, and in practice the vendor is free not to reduce any prices and still remain faithful to the wording of the advertisement.

Weasel words can imply meaning far beyond the claim actually being made. Some weasel words may also have the effect of softening the force of a potentially loaded or otherwise controversial statement through some form of understatement, for example using words such as 'somewhat' or 'in most respects'.

In the English language, commands end with a down-turn in tonality. Embedded commands require the use of a commanding tonality to be effective. These commands usually possess the word formation of a question, but the tonality of a command. For example: 'What's it like when you become incredibly loving!'

The purpose of using embedded commands is to move the mind of the recipient in the direction you want it to go without seeming to be intruding or ordering in any way.

Combine the weasel phrase with a command verb, like 'get', 'become', 'experience', 'remember', etc. Bolt on the state, process or experience you want the other person to have, and you've got your embedded command. The formula is:

Weasel phrases
+ command verbs
+ states, processes or experiences
+ **commanding tonality**
= embedded commands

Here are the most important and useful weasel phrases. We will use each one to embed the command, 'feel incredibly loving'.

1. **When you …** 'When you' presupposes that the person is going to do the thing or experience the state you describe, so it's no longer open to debate or doubt. 'When you feel incredibly loving, do you find yourself compelled to act on it?'

2. **What would it be like if …?** This weasel phrase is, in effect, a command for the person to imagine the

condition or occurrence named or described after it. 'What would it be like if you were to feel incredibly loving?'

3. **A person can ...** Talking about 'a person' deflects any resistance on the part of the recipient, since you really aren't talking about him or her. 'A person can feel incredibly loving, talking with someone they really, really like!'

4. **If you were to ...** By saying 'if,' it deflects resistance while directing the person to imagine the experience, condition, feeling or situation you're describing. 'If you were to feel incredibly loving, do you think you might feel compelled to act on it?'

5. **As you ...** This phrase assumes that the person will do the behaviour or undergo the condition you describe. 'As you feel incredibly loving, can you feel how excited you're getting?'

6. **It's not necessary to ...** By saying it isn't necessary, it eliminates any resistance, since you're saying they don't really have to do it (even though they will!). 'It's not necessary to feel incredibly loving, as you listen carefully to what I say!'

7. **You really shouldn't ...** Since you're saying they 'shouldn't', it's not like you're trying to get them to do anything, are you? 'You really shouldn't ... feel incredibly loving!'

8. **You might find ...** Useful as the start of an intensifying chain of phrases. It implies that they're going to experience what you describe as something that just happens, so it's not like you're commanding them to do it. 'You might find as you feel incredibly loving, that it could lead to your acting on it!'

9. **To the point where ...** This phrase connects one thing the recipient is experiencing with the next thing you want them to experience, so it's useful both as a connector and an amplifier. 'You might find those pictures start to get bigger and brighter to the point where you feel incredibly loving!'

10. **Invite you to notice ...** This has the same effect as 'you might find' because it implies that what you describe is going to happen. Plus, 'invite' has pleasant connotations of it being voluntary and polite. 'And I invite you to notice how the warmth of my voice can allow you to feel incredibly loving!'

11. **How surprised would you be to ...** This implies that the event you describe is certainly going to happen, and the only question is how surprised they'll be by it. An example is: 'How surprised would you be to find that you can feel incredibly loving?'

By using these basic building blocks, you'll be able to create virtually any and all states you want to create, very rapidly, in the people you really want to persuade.

How to use embedded commands

When you're in normal, everyday conversations you can influence people to watch the film you want to watch, accept your suggestion, do the dishes, get them to sell their house, sign the contract, or whatever else you want them to do with absolutely no resistance.

How is there no resistance? Because embedded commands bypass conscious reasoning and speak directly to you at a subconscious level. People simply begin to get it in their minds that they should do whatever it is you want them to do. Embedded commands are one-to-four-word groups that order you to do something, and they make sense on their own.

Powerful embedded commands

When I run a seminar, I usually begin by using some embedded commands to prepare the delegates for action.

For example: 'Usually my delegates *do as I say*. Shall we *begin*?'

As I would usually have asked a number of questions that they would all have responded to positively, everyone always answers affirmatively. Internally, the delegates may be thinking: 'Did he just say I had to do what he said?'

And here's an example my trainer used on me during marathon training: 'If you don't *train every day*, you'll struggle when it comes to marathon day. Don't you agree?'

The inflection is on 'train every day'. Even though it's structured in the form of a question, you've included the answer: 'Yes, you do agree.' *Train every day* is the embedded command.

Further examples include:

- 'You should let me coach you, so I can help you get what you want.' *Let me coach you* is the command.
- 'You must take notes while I'm speaking. You'll learn so much more. Shall we do that now?' *Take notes* is the embedded command.
- 'You can begin to relax now that you're here.' *Begin to relax* is the embedded command.
- 'You need to think deeply about what you're saying.' *Think deeply* is the embedded command.
- 'I don't know when you'll feel motivated.' *Feel motivated* is the embedded command.

 Follow these four rules to incorporate embedded commands into your phrases:

1. Pause before the embedded command.
2. Go louder on the embedded command.
3. Down-turn in tonality on the embedded command.
4. Pause after the embedded command.

TRY IT NOW! Make a list of embedded commands and practise incorporating them into regular conversations. Examples include:

- Sign the contract
- Trust me
- Accept this offer
- Work with me
- Decide now
- Act now
- Do what I say
- Do as I say
- Feel motivated
- Get excited
- Take action
- Agree with me
- Convince yourself
- Believe me
- Extend the deadline
- Come to my office
- Sign this now
- Listen to me
- Accept less
- Take notes

Uses, abuses and benefits of embedded commands

Embedded commands will not automatically make any-one do what you want them to do. However, by the nature of how they work, the recipient will have to think about the focus of the command, however briefly. What they do from there is up to them, but you will have embedded the thought into their heads.

These are the key uses and benefits of embedded commands:

Control how the masses think

Politicians use embedded commands in their speech con-tinually. In a speech by Tony Blair a few years ago, he con-tinually used the phrase: 'We, like America, need to …' Needless to say, at the time, support in the UK for American foreign policy was low and Blair wanted to change that. If you can embed commands directly into your speeches, presentations and conversations, just how much more can you move people the way you want them to go? How much would you want to learn about how to do this?

Accidentally embedded headaches

Recently I was listening to two women talking while on a plane to New York. One woman complained about a head-ache and then (unintentionally) spent the next ten minutes using embedded commands to install the same headache in her friend. I only overheard the conversation and even I began to develop a headache. If she could do this by accident, imagine what people might wilfully be doing to us.

Booking business meetings
When Dee joined our sales team she was tasked with re-engaging lapsed clients through telesales. After a couple of days of non-committal responses, lots of frustration and many hours on the phone, she asked for my help. I changed two words in her script and got her to use command tonality with her voice. In short, we changed two sentences from weak questions to strong embedded commands. The next day she got four appointments from eight calls.

Getting dates
A friend of a friend who I met at an event was telling us he had just proposed. I asked him how he had met his partner. His response was online dating, and out of curiosity I asked about his experience with it. He said that he had struggled for years with not attracting the right people and for long periods he wasn't receiving any contacts from his profile at all. Then a coach suggested he change a sentence in his online dating profile to read: 'Only contact me if you want …', and he bullet-pointed a list of benefit statements about dating him. He got more contacts on the day he made the change than he had the three months before – and one of them happened to be his future fiancée!

Making sales

Think about embedded commands and see how many there are in the following sentence:

'Before you consider buying, let's talk about the benefits so you can make the right decision – that way you can buy with confidence.'

I've deliberately not marked out the voice intonation so you have to get this for yourself. Once you've got at least three, just imagine how powerful a simple sentence like this can be – and what will happen when you begin constructing and delivering these kind of commands yourself.

 Other people are using them on you

Advertisers, sales professionals and politicians all know about these ideas and aren't shy of using them. A quick trawl around the internet will give you hundreds of examples from Tony Blair to Barack Obama, from internet marketers to TV advertising. Even if you don't want to use them on other people, you need to learn about embedded commands to understand how they're being used on you.

Creating a Toolkit

13. Goal-setting

Goal-setting is a prerequisite to success in most areas of life. Yet 95% of people still don't set goals.

The NLP model enables us to go beyond mere goal-setting into the actual programming of our minds to drive us towards our desired goal.

The brain works primarily from our sensory system (pictures, sounds, feelings). The NLP goal-setting model addresses this by getting our goal to be **sensory-specific**. But it doesn't stop there. For the brain not only uses the sensory system, it also uses our **word meanings** that drive the sensory system. For this reason, the NLP goal-setting model makes absolutely sure that we use language ourselves in such a way as to drive our very neurology and physiology towards obtaining our desired goal.

The NLP goal-setting model helps you to concentrate on what you internally see, hear, and feel. Your attention will direct itself towards external and internal resources necessary for achieving the goal.

The NLP model provides the following key components that enable you to effectively identify your desired outcome – and it begins by eliciting that outcome immediately:

1. State the goal in positive terms.
2. Specify the goal in sensory-based terms.
3. Specify the goal in a way that you find compelling.
4. Run a quality control (ecology) check on the goal to ensure balance in all areas of your home/work life.
5. Ensure that the goal can be self-initiated and maintained.
6. State the context of the goal.
7. State the resources needed to achieve the goal.
8. How will you evidence success?

The goal-setting process

Defining our goals

Firstly we must recognize and define our goals. The six-step process below is a method for formulating a goal and then checking to ascertain if the goal will work.

1. Where do you want to be, or what do you want to achieve? Answer this question against each goal.
2. How will you know when you have succeeded?
3. What will the effects be on you and those around you?
4. What resources do you need to succeed? Do you have the resources or access to the resources?
5. What has prevented you from doing anything about this before? How can you stop it happening this time?
6. Final check – is this all you can achieve, want or desire?

Clarifying our goals

A useful tool for clarifying our goals is the 'SMARTO' framework:

S – Specific: 'To be happier' is non-specific, indefinable and impossible to quantify. 'To get up at 6.30 instead of 7.30, so that I can be in the office an hour earlier' is specific.

M – Measurable: It's impossible to tell if the goal has been achieved if it can't be measured. It's also encouraging, especially as the goal may take some time to achieve fully, if the progress towards the goal can be measured.

A – Achievable: The goal has to be realistic. Attempting a goal that isn't clearly achievable will only result in disappointment. It's pointless for someone with a numeracy problem to enrol on a degree course in mathematics. By adjusting the goal to enrolling in numeracy classes, you're attempting something with a realistic chance of success, which may or may not lead to a desire for further achievement.

R – Realistic/Relevant: The goal must be relevant to you and your situation. Going for long walks in the countryside may be enjoyable, but it's hardly relevant for someone who is trying to meet new people.

T – Time: There must be a specific period over which either all, or a specific part of the goal, will be achieved. If goals are likely to take too long, they should be broken down into stages, so that you can see quite clearly how far you have progressed.

O – Own: The goal MUST be your own, otherwise it's unlikely to succeed or sustain.

The SOFI goal analysis tool
SOFI stands for **Strengths**, **Options**, **Fears** and **Impediments**.

Let's take, for example, the goal of running the London Marathon in April next year, and put it through the SOFI process:

What are your strengths?
What can you do, or what do you already do, that will help you to achieve this goal?
- I enjoy being outdoors
- I'm in relatively good shape
- I have friends/family that run
- I'm enthusiastic and motivated.

What are the options available to you to achieve this goal?
- There's a local running club that I can join
- I can subscribe to a web forum for advice
- I can purchase a running magazine/book
- I could join a gym
- I can rope a friend into running/training with me
- I could sign up with a personal trainer.

What scares you about this goal?
- I may fail to achieve it
- I may embarrass myself
- I'm not a runner
- People might laugh at me.

What impedes me from achieving this goal?
- Time available to train
- The demands of my family
- I have a very busy workload
- I'm too tired to train
- I can't afford the proper equipment (shoes, clothing etc.).

Once a goal has been through the SOFI process, all the hidden reasons for not achieving the goal tend to come to the surface. This enables you to challenge, support or encourage yourself towards goal accomplishment.

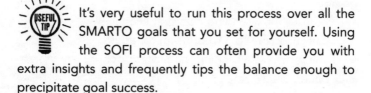 It's very useful to run this process over all the SMARTO goals that you set for yourself. Using the SOFI process can often provide you with extra insights and frequently tips the balance enough to precipitate goal success.

Four steps to success

There are four essential steps to getting what you want. They are simple, yet profound. **They are the basis of all human success, and the foundation of NLP.**

If you're committed to achieving your desires, these steps are sufficient, even without further support or explanation, to make significant changes in your life. When reinforced with the specific NLP principles and techniques described in this book, they provide all the technology you need to get what you want.

1. Know your outcome

NLP focuses on knowing your outcome – the result that you want to achieve. Any successful person knows what he or she wants. This is what marks out achievers. If you're not particularly ambitious or goal-orientated, it might not seem natural to state your goals in a specific way. But you can start somewhere. We all have wishes and dreams, including those that will ultimately benefit family and friends or the wider community. There may be habits you want to change, or skills and abilities you admire in others that you would like to have yourself. All these can be expressed as what NLP calls outcomes, enabling you to become a goal-achieving person. Having clearly expressed outcomes gives you the maximum chance of fulfilling them.

2. Take action

Do what you think will bring about the achievement of your desire. This sounds very obvious, but the main characteristic of high achievers is that they actually start to do the things that others just talk and dream about. What you do might not always work, so there's an element of personal risk. However, you will never know what you're capable of until you take action.

3. Pay attention to the results of your action

This requires what's called 'sensory acuity', as we saw in Chapter 7. You need to be able to observe accurately the things that happen as a result of your behaviour – whether your actions are bringing you nearer to achieving your outcome. You also need to spot the signals, or negative feedback, that show when you're off course. Much of NLP is concerned with understanding how we sense things, interpret them, and feed the information back into further actions.

4. Keep adjusting your course until you arrive at your destination

Be prepared to change your approach and behaviour until you get the results you desire. Based on sensory feedback, you must always be ready to do something else. If at first you don't succeed, try something different! Sometimes this requires creative thinking on your part.

Because these four steps are so simple, there's a danger of overlooking them and seeking something far more demanding and complex. Another common mistake is to miss out one stage – such as being willing to do something even when you're not sure exactly what result it will bring, or being willing to change your behaviour when you'd prefer to stay with a more predictable, risk-free way of behaving. But if you spend time observing people who have done worthwhile things with their lives, including people you know well, you'll begin to see this pattern of important steps in every success they achieve.

THINK ABOUT IT These simple steps are sometimes demanding, at least initially, but there's always a price to pay for getting anything worthwhile. Be assured that your investment will be repaid many times over – and as with other demanding activities, there can be almost as much pleasure in the journey as in reaching the destination.

Goal-setting summary

- Successful people set goals
- Goals take you from where you are to where you want to be
- A goal is anything you want or need

- You need to consider other goals, other people and other aspects of your life when setting your goals
- When you do this, you set **smart goals**.

Answer the following questions related to your goal, using the information and examples given to help you.

1. **What do you want?**
   Check that your goal is: a) stated positively; b) measurable; c) time-limited.

2. **Where, when and with whom?**
   Define the context in which you want your goal.

3. **How will you know success?**
   When you're clear about your evidence, you'll know when you've achieved your goal.

4. **What resources can you use?**
   Which of your experiences, friends, personal qualities and role models will you use to help you achieve your goal?

5. **What is the cost of achieving your goal?**
   Consider your time, money and effort.

6. **How will others be affected?**
   Who else is involved? What will change?

7. **What are the consequences?**
   What else could happen as a result of achieving your goal?

8. **Keep which present benefits?**
   How can you keep the benefits you get currently from not having your goal and not working towards it?

9. **What actions will you take?**
   Determine the actions needed; refine them; secure the help of others; take action.

10. **Does the goal feel right?**
    Go back and review your goal.

The secrets of success

- Know what you really want
- Set your goal
- Take action
- Notice the results you're actually achieving
- Be flexible enough to change what you are doing to get your goal
- This goal is unlikely to be isolated from the rest of your life.

Consider

- Which larger goal does this one support?
- Which smaller goals are helpful in achieving this one?

Platinum goal-setting with the seven-step achievement plan

Only 5% of people who set New Year resolutions are successful in maintaining them – that's a whopping 95% failure rate. This is because most people don't understand the steps you must follow to achieve sustainable long-term results – and as a result never get off the starting block.

This plan will guide you through the process, giving you the perfect way to create the momentum that will compel you to continue on the path to a phenomenal year filled with success, achievement and fulfilment!

First step: Be clear

First, you must clarify where you really are now …

1. **What did you love about last year?**
   a) What were your magic moments? When were you larger than life? When did you surprise yourself? What did you achieve that was truly outstanding and extraordinary?
   b) What were your accomplishments in the last year?
   c) What are some of the things from the last year that you wish to replicate in the next year?

2. **What did you hate about last year?**
   a) What did you find challenging about last year?
   b) What things that happened in the last year (or before) do you wish to avoid happening in the next year, or ever again?

    c) What learning did you gain by going through these experiences?

    d) Why was this learning valuable to you?

3. **What decisions did you make in the last year that empowered you?**

    a) What were the most important decisions that you made last year?

    b) What decisions will you make in the next year as a result?

Second step: Be certain

Now we know where you are, it's time to create the certainty that you have the ability to turn your dreams into reality.

1. Make a list of anything in your life that was once merely a dream, goal, wish or desire. Think of some of the massive things and even some of the smaller ambitions that at one time seemed difficult or even completely impossible, yet you somehow managed to achieve, attain or acquire.

2. Mark three items from the above list that were the most difficult for you to achieve.

3. For the three items you marked, write down what process you went through to turn each one of them into reality. It was probably not a conscious act, but there's

a good possibility that something made you desire it so much it became a fantastic obsession for you. At this point did you find that you were continuously focused on it? Put a lot of emotional charge into it? Then what? Did you actually create a plan? What were the steps you followed?

Third step: Be excited

Now that you've identified and clarified where it is that you've been, and you're certain about your ability to make your goals, dreams and desires come true, it's time to decide where you want to go …

1. In an optimal state of awareness (jump around, dance, anything to get the blood flowing to your head), list every goal you'd like to accomplish in the next 20 years. Ensure that you include ANYTHING you want to do, be, share, create, have and give. Consider physical goals, career goals, financial goals, personal development goals, relationship goals, contribution goals – anything you would like to learn, enjoy, experience, achieve or do. No matter how ridiculous, unrealistic or outrageous it may seem, this is your chance to dream without limits. Be sure to keep your pen moving as fast as possible!

2. When you're done, review your list, and next to each goal write down the number of years you would like it to take (or believe it will take) to achieve your goal: 1 year, 2–3 years, 5 years, 10 years or 20 years.

Fourth step: Be focused

From your list of goals from the third step, mark your top four goals that you believe will take a year to achieve. Out of your entire list, what do you want most? What are the top four goals that, if you could achieve them this year, would get you up at the crack of dawn and keep you burning the midnight oil with excitement?

Fifth step: Be committed

1. Think of your top four one-year goals and devise a statement (a few sentences) about why they're 'MUST DO'. For what reason will you achieve this no matter what? Remember, reasons come first, answers come second! What makes you want to do this?

2. Think of some of the things that you may be required to do *that you don't particularly want to do* in order to achieve these goals. If you have enough passion, you can get yourself to do anything, but first you must be certain about what 'anything' might entail. Let's face up to our fears and look the beast in the eye!

Sixth step: Be driven

IMPERATIVE! Never leave the goal-setting moment without taking action towards its achievement. You must take *massive* immediate action. It's the first step of your journey …

1. Decide NOW: What are some small things that you will do *immediately* towards achieving one of your top goals (e.g. making a phone call, booking a meeting, getting on the internet to research, signing up for a seminar, getting a coach, getting advice, support or training)?

2. What big things do you resolve to do *immediately* to achieve this goal (e.g. making a decision, throwing out all the unhealthy food in your house right now, giving something away, etc.)?

Seventh step: Be smart

To ensure you follow through, you have to get smart and measure yourself consistently. Remember, most people set some form of New Year goal, yet have no plan or direction, take no action, and then measure again next New Year! The more you measure something, the better it gets. You must resolve now to measure your specific progress daily, or at least weekly.

How will you measure your progress? You could find a mentor or coach, keep a diary, announce your plans on your blog/website/channel for maximum accountability, then blog about your progress or record a progress video to upload.

14. Visualization

*It is only through imagination that men become aware
of what the world might be.*

Bertrand Russell

Much of how people experience and construct the world is based on what they experience **visually**. It follows, then, that if you want to change how your reality is constructed, a good start would be with a visualization of a different reality.

Visualization is the process of using your imagination to create mental images, and it's used by NLP to program and change behaviour. Combined with positive thinking, visualization can be a powerful tool in achieving your goals.

 Our subconscious can't differentiate between what's real and what's perceived, and if we can create something vividly enough subconsciously, it becomes very real for us – and even our bodies will react to accommodate the new reality.

Visualization and imagination in NLP

NLP uses a number of techniques involving visualization, from requiring subjects to visualize where they want to be in ten years (imagining themselves as they want to be) to using visualization to reinforce confidence and self-assurance. Visualization may be used to create dreams, imagine outcomes, and help people achieve desired results.

Using your imagination to create mental images stimulates focus and self-organization, and points attention in a particular direction, allowing the unconscious mind to work towards the image created. Visualization can be used in the creation of a desired life if one is able to practise it effectively.

Be careful what you wish for

A common slogan used by NLP practitioners and in self-help books is 'be careful what you wish for'. The close link between visualization and the unconscious mind makes it not only powerful, but dangerous.

If you were to visualize a negative outcome, this would enable the achievement of that outcome. The unconscious mind doesn't distinguish between negative and positive visualizations: use it wisely!

How to imagine effectively

Effective visualization in NLP involves using a combination of **memory** and **fantasy** in the creation of positive mental images for the purpose of focusing your conscious and unconscious mind on a particular goal. As noted above, the mind can't tell the difference between a real-life event and a vividly imagined one.

CASE STUDY

If you read an enthralling passage in a book about a man fighting for his life against a lion in the African savannah, and imagine the man's fight vividly, you'll find your heart rate rising, perhaps some sweat forming on your brow, and your physiology responding in much the same way as the man in the story. This is testament to the mind's inability to distinguish between the real and imagined.

In NLP, effective visualization is achieved in the present: that is, you need to visualize achieving your dreams **in the now**. Visualize how you would feel, what emotions you would experience, how other people would respond to you, and how you would look, among other things. The key to effective visualization is to create as detailed, clear and vivid a picture as possible to focus on. The more vivid the visualization, the more likely, and quickly, you will begin to attract the things to help you achieve your desired outcomes through your subconscious mind.

Harnessing the imagination

By using our imagination and creating mental images, we stimulate and alert our neurology to a particular direction, triggering self-organizing processes that begin to automatically and unconsciously work towards achieving the outcomes we have imaged. As the old mantra says: 'Energy flows where attention goes.' When we imagine a goal or dream in our mind's eye, it allows us to recognize and mobilize the resources necessary to turn imagination into reality – what Walt Disney called 'imagineering'.

Visualization is often used by sport psychologists to help improve athletic performance. Numerous examples exist of how visualizing has promoted the increased development of physical skills.

In one study, gymnasts who were to learn a new move were divided into two groups. One group was instructed to visualize themselves being able to do this particular move, while the other group was given no instructions. A couple of weeks later, when the time came for them to do this particular move, without the benefit of any previous physical practice, the group who visualized had a 50% to 60% success rate, whereas the group that had not visualized had only about 10% success initially.

In another example, a soccer team was split into two groups in order to practise free kicks. One group physically practised taking the free kicks. The other group was instructed to sit on the benches and mentally practise by visualizing that they were taking the free kicks. When the two groups competed with each other to see who performed better, those players who visualized were more successful at scoring from free kicks than the group who had actually practised.

Imagination is also necessary to create and understand symbols and metaphors, and to provide motivation and meaning for our present actions. According to Albert Einstein: 'Imagination is more important than knowledge.' Einstein claimed that knowledge of the past and present was essentially 'dead', and required imagination to bring it to life and put knowledge into action. As novelist H.G. Wells maintained: 'All youth lives much in reverie, thereby the stronger minds rehearse themselves for life in a thousand imaginations.'

Imagination and imagery

Imagination is clearly based on our ability to create mental imagery. From the NLP perspective, images are considered one of the primary building blocks of a person's model of the world. In particular, imagery is often used to define desired dreams, visions and outcomes. As Aristotle put it:

When the mind is actively aware of anything, it is necessarily aware of it along with an image ... To the thinking soul, images serve as if they were contents of perception ... just as if it were seeing, it calculates and deliberates what is to come by reference to what is present; and when it makes a pronouncement, as in the case of sensation it pronounces the object to be pleasant or painful, in this case it avoids or pursues.

On the Soul

According to Aristotle, we construct a mental map ('image') of the future from associations drawn from ongoing sensory experience. The mind then 'calculates and deliberates' by 'seeing' or constructing mental images of 'what is to come by reference to what is present', through memory and imagination. It's this internal map that determines whether we will perceive an object or situation to be 'pleasant or painful'.

THINK ABOUT IT Because it's produced by the body's nervous system, imagery can also influence the body in several ways. Often, images of goals and outcomes form a focal point or **attractor** around which behaviour becomes self-organized. In hypnotic work, imagery (often in the form of symbols and metaphors) is used as a means to understand and direct unconscious activity and create trance states, usually through the method of 'guided fantasy'. Imagery can also influence the function of the autonomic nervous system. Mental images, for instance, have been used to stimulate immune system functioning and other healing processes. There are therapists who have incorporated visualization as one of the main components in the treatment of cancer.

Mental rehearsal

Some time ago, a study was made of people who had survived airline accidents. They were asked how they had managed to get free of the wreckage, with so much chaos going on, while many of their fellow passengers did not. It's an interesting question, because escaping an air crash isn't something you get much chance to practise. How do you prepare yourself to do something you've never done before?

The most common answer to this question was that they had run a kind of mental 'dress rehearsal' over and over in their minds. They would visualize the sequence of undoing their safety belt, moving out of their seat, going down the aisle to the nearest exit, jumping down the slide, etc. They would repeat this sequence over and over, feeling themselves doing what they saw in their visualization, until it seemed that they had already done this activity many times before. Then, after the accident, when there was total havoc, they didn't need to waste any time or conscious awareness thinking about what to do. The program was already in place. One of these people even mentioned that after the crash, he found himself going out of the exit and suddenly realized he could hear the person who had been sitting next to him screaming that he couldn't get his seat belt off.

Mental rehearsal relates to our ability to practise a process or activity in our minds. In NLP, mental rehearsal is used to strengthen or improve behavioural performance, cognitive thinking patterns and internal states. For example, when applied to behavioural performance, mental rehearsal involves creating internal representations, in the form of images, sounds and feelings, of some behaviour or performance we desire to enact or improve (as an actor might silently rehearse lines for a play).

At the level of behavioural performance, there are several different strategies for mental rehearsal. The mental rehearsal of a particular activity may be done from either an **associated** or **dissociated** perspective – for example, imagining a situation from one's own perspective or watching oneself from the point of view of an observer, as if watching oneself in a movie or video.

THINK ABOUT IT

Mental rehearsal done from an associated perspective is like entering a 'virtual reality' and becoming an actor in a play or movie. From a dissociated perspective, mental rehearsal allows a person to be more like the editor or director of the play or movie. Thus, when done from an associated perspective, mental rehearsal can be used in order to internalize, or 'install', a particular behaviour. When done from a dissociated perceptual position, mental rehearsal can be used to anticipate possible consequences of a particular action in a situation (its ecological impact or appropriateness, for instance), as a type of mental simulation.

In order to actually internalize a behaviour, mental rehearsal is typically more effective when done from an associated perspective. The most direct form is to simply project oneself into a future situation, and imagine delivering the desired performance. To mentally rehearse a speech, for instance, you would imagine being in the future situation, and create a multi-sensory representation of the way you would like to perform. As you mentally rehearse giving an effective and compelling speech, you would imagine what you would be seeing in that situation, feeling the movements and expressions of your body, and hearing what your voice would sound like as you gave the speech.

Other strategies include the New Behaviour Generator strategy, in which key elements of the desired performance are first described verbally. The linguistic description forms the basis for constructing a *dissociated* visual image of the desired actions. You then imagine enacting the performance you have fantasized from an *associated* position, and check your feelings of confidence and congruence about doing the imagined behaviour. If there are any doubts, you return to the verbal description and either add to it or refine it.

Future pacing

Mental rehearsal is a key element of many NLP techniques. In fact, a form of mental rehearsal called **future pacing**, in which a person imagines enacting changes in behaviour in specific contexts, is a final step in practically every NLP intervention.

Future pacing is a type of mental imagery, a powerful way to connect changes in behaviour to future situations or a particular event (such as a sporting performance). Usually we do future pacing at the end of an NLP process to ensure that these changes are available outside in the everyday world. It's easy to respond resourcefully when there's no immediate threat or pressure!

By imagining and virtually experiencing situations where you would appropriately use the change in behaviour, you can find out if it's triggered automatically. For instance, imagine walking in the front door and seeing chaos – does your 'calm and patient' resource kick in? What are you saying to yourself? How are you breathing and feeling?

When doing this for someone else, you need to consider:

- Do they look calm and patient?
- What is their body language and breathing like?
- What is their voice tone and volume like?
- Do they sound or look tense, like they did when they described their previous, unwanted, response?

Future pacing test

1. Think of four possible situations in the future that would have previously triggered the old behaviour that you are seeking to modify. For example, seeing a mess in the living room, getting a phone call from the teacher, a colleague letting you down, etc.
2. Imagine stepping into the first situation. See, hear, feel (as in touch, not emotion), smell and/or taste what you would experience in this first situation, that is associated to the context.
3. Does the change hold? Do you respond in the way you would like?
4. Consider if you need to make further changes to fine-tune the desired response.
5. Repeat steps 2 to 4 for the other three situations.
6. Come back to now, and imagine and see yourself (dissociated) in the future with the changes you have made.

Everyday uses for visualization

For lots of things in life a good visual skill is essential, and we all have the ability to visualize.

• Imagine being a hairdresser who didn't know what a haircut was going to look like before they started

- Imagine being a taxi driver who couldn't picture where he was going
- Imagine being an architect, builder or carpenter who didn't know what the finished item would look like
- Imagine being an artist who had no idea what they were painting or sculpting
- Imagine being a surveyor who had no idea whether the building matched the plans.

 Ten steps for goal-setting

1. Have goals for all areas of your life – business, professional, career, family, health, finances, etc.

2. Include both short- and long-term goals.

3. Write down your goals so they become more than just a wish. There's growing evidence to show that writing down your goals makes you 50% more likely to achieve them.

4. State your goals in the positive:
   - What do you want?
   - What will that do for you?

5. Visualize yourself achieving your goals. Visualize your success by vividly imagining and seeing yourself accomplishing your goals.

6. Define specifically what the outcome will be, involving all the senses:

- How will you know that you have achieved it?
- What will you be seeing when you have achieved it?
- What will you be hearing when you have achieved it?
- What will you be feeling when you have achieved it?
- What will someone else see you doing when you've achieved it?
- What will you hear yourself saying when you've achieved it?

7. Ensure you have the resources you need.

8. When do you want to achieve your goals? Have a clearly defined time-frame.

9. Establish the first step you need to take, and then decide on the next steps.

10. When are you going to start? Confirm a date or time when you will start.

REMEMBER THIS!!!

Realizing and visualizing your goals

Using your senses and your imagination can have a powerful effect on making your goals realistic and compelling. The more details you can add, as if it's happening now, the more powerful and effective the technique is in turning your goals into reality. Be clear what you want and what obstacles you may need to overcome. 'See' and 'experience' your outcome as if it exists already – then you will have created a compelling goal.

---

15. Anchoring

The ability to create and **anchor** powerful states is one of the most useful and effective of all NLP techniques. How would it impact on your life if you knew you could give your very best performance in everything you did, and every time you did it? Every job interview, every presentation, every exam, every sporting performance a complete success. Imagine what your life would be like if you knew that every outcome would be a positive one.

So what is an NLP anchor?

The concept of anchoring in NLP is the ability to access the most powerful, the most appropriate state for a particular activity, event or task, and then being able to get into that state at will.

An anchor is a **stimulus** that reminds you of events and can change your state positively or negatively. The stimulus can involve all the senses (e.g. something you see, hear, feel, taste or smell) and it can be internal or external.

An **internal** anchor is generated in your mind, for example as you remember a visual image that evokes certain feelings. An **external** anchor can be triggered when, for example, you hear a piece of music that reminds you of a lovely holiday or experience.

If we experience an external state or create an internal state that is real and vivid, we can trick ourselves into thinking we're actually experiencing it. Smells and tastes are particularly powerful anchors: the smell of freshly baked apple pie may remind you of your grandmother, or a perfume may remind you of a particular person. You may associate the taste of piña colada with being relaxed on holiday. Regardless of your age, you're likely to have smells or tastes that evoke the feeling and memory of something from your childhood.

NLP defines anchoring as an internal or external representation that will trigger another representation. It's the natural process by which one element or sensory component of an event recreates the whole experience. It relies on what's known as the **stimulus–response** concept, where a particular stimulus will elicit a memory, behaviour or feeling. Some of these responses are beyond our awareness.

For example, when we approach a traffic signal and see the amber light turn on, we slow down. When we see the red light turn on, we immediately put our foot on the brake. Over time, this becomes an unconscious process and is triggered whenever we see the traffic signal.

 By being aware of how we set anchors in others and in ourselves, we can take control of the process. We can then set positive anchors in ourselves and in others, so that we can achieve an outcome or create an environment of excellence.

145

We create an anchor representation every time we communicate with another person: we use sounds and visual symbols to represent an experience, or to trigger past memories, feelings, ideas, thoughts and representations. Good communicators always use anchoring techniques to attach states, representations and experiences.

When can I use NLP anchoring techniques?
When you feel unhappy or in a negative frame of mind, you can create a more resourceful state by triggering positive anchors in your mind and body. You can also create positive anchors for a future situation that is causing you concern.

The majority of people use one specific sense, usually **touch**, for most of their NLP anchors, simply because it's the easiest way to re-access them.

One of the most important aspects of setting up an anchor is to start by creating the strongest state possible. This will determine the strength of the anchor. A weak state results in a weak anchor!

Developing the art of effective anchoring
Anchoring happens all the time in our lives, and it's not a new concept. It's just that we don't realize that anchoring is taking place. Therefore anchoring usually occurs outside our conscious awareness. When we come across a trigger, all our representational systems are activated.

Creating a confidence anchor

One of the easiest and most useful anchors we can create is for **confidence**.

Begin by thinking of a time when you were supremely confident, a time when you performed at your very best and may even have amazed yourself. If for any reason you can't think of a time when you were confident, then imagine what it would be like if you were supremely confident.

Once you've remembered that experience, think of it in the present tense as if you were back there again experiencing it for the first time.

Think about:

1. Where you are
2. What you're doing
3. Who you're with
4. What images and colours do you see?
5. What do you hear?
6. How do you feel (other than supremely confident, of course)?
7. Are you aware of any smells or tastes that you associate with this experience?

The key is to make this state as powerful as you possibly can.

Begin by finding the visual submodalities that made a feeling or sensation stronger for you, and apply them to the experience of you being confident.

147

Be sure to incorporate the auditory submodalities too. If you find that volume has a positive effect, be sure to turn it up, as this can make the feeling stronger.

Once you've achieved a strong feeling, then be aware of how the feeling moves through your body, and let the feeling build and grow stronger and stronger as it moves.

As you focus and concentrate the feeling, as you continue to change the submodalities, take one of your hands and squeeze your thumb and forefinger together, and continue squeezing firmly while you continue to revivify that feeling of supreme confidence. As you squeeze more firmly, be aware of the feeling becoming stronger and stronger.

Keep squeezing until you feel that you're in the strongest, most confident state you can create.

Now go and refocus yourself, make a cup of tea, go for a walk, or just focus on something else for at least five minutes.

We now have a strong anchor, so it's important for us to test that it works.

Take the same hand and squeeze the thumb and forefinger together again. Be aware of the changes that occur. If you find that you haven't re-accessed the confident state, then start the process again. Keep going through the process until you test an anchor that connects you to the confident state.

You'll be clearly aware when you've created an effective anchor, as the changes will be easy to notice.

This is one of the simplest forms of anchoring, and we can use the same process to create any state.

Modalities and submodalities

We have five basic senses: visual, auditory, kinaesthetic (touch), olfactory (smell) and gustatory (taste). In NLP, these are referred to as representational systems or **modalities**. For each of these modalities, we can have finer distinctions. We could describe a picture as being black and white or colour, or it could also be bright or dim. Sounds could be loud or soft, or coming from a particular direction. Feelings could be in different parts of the body or have different temperatures. Smells could be pleasant or offensive, strong or light. Taste could be sweet or bitter or strong or mild. These finer distinctions are called **submodalities**, and they define the qualities of our internal representations. Generally, NLP works with only three modalities: visual, auditory and kinaesthetic.

Types of anchors

Anchors can be visual, auditory or kinaesthetic.

Visual anchors

You can use visual anchors to anchor a state. You can use external or internal anchors. For example, I have a crystal on a necklace that I have anchored for success and achievement. In order for this to be effective, the external anchor always has to be available for you to use. You may find it relaxing and calming to view a certain landscape, but unless you can carry it around with you, it's of limited value. You can, however, use an internal image of the landscape to anchor your resourceful feeling.

Most visual anchors are internal. Some examples of visual anchors are:

- Symbols – for example, you could use a circle as a symbol for being calm and relaxed and anchor this to your state
- People, such as a trusted friend or mentor – or even a person from history or current affairs
- Various objects and landscapes can be used as anchors for being calm and relaxed – for example, you could imagine:
  a) A beautiful beach
  b) A summer garden
  c) Your childhood teddy bear or doll.

Auditory anchors

You can use a sound as an anchor. Like visual anchors, sounds can be internal or external. Many people have used whistling or humming as an anchor. You can use an internal voice as an anchor. For example, you could anchor the affirmation: 'I am calm and relaxed.'

Kinaesthetic anchors

Examples of kinaesthetic anchors are:

- Imagining a comforting hand on your shoulder
- Squeezing the thumb and forefinger as we did earlier
- Touching yourself on the hand or other unobtrusive place – you can choose a point and treat it like an acupressure point, pressing on it to fire the required state.

 You can use a combination of visual, kinaesthetic and auditory anchors, such as seeing a certain symbol in your mind's eye, hearing something said (for example, 'Calm and relaxed'), and pressing your hand in a special place.

Anchors can be created anywhere on your body. You don't need to squeeze finger and thumb together – pressing a knuckle or earlobe works equally well. The only things to bear in mind when choosing a location for an anchor are that it's accessible (and appropriate!) when you're planning to fire it, that the location is specific (pressing your upper thigh isn't specific), and that the more nerves there are in the area you use for the anchor, the more successful it's likely to be.

 A fascinating use for anchoring has been to create an anchor during sexual intercourse. At the point of orgasm, squeeze a partner's shoulder or earlobe to anchor the sensation.

Then, the next time they're doing the dishes, fire the anchor and see what happens!

You could also try creating eight different states on the fingers of both hands, and then firing them one after the other.

The four keys to anchoring

The anchoring technique isn't complex, but you need to follow a few systematic and precise steps. There are four keys for performing anchoring:

1. Uniqueness

In order to set a permanent anchor in another person, a unique stimulus must be used. A stimulus such as shaking hands can't be used as an anchor, as it's a general behaviour. When a stimulus or location is so unique that it can't be found in our daily lives, it's the best type of trigger possible for setting an anchor that lasts for a long time.

In the case of using kinaesthetic anchors, identify all the aspects of the stimulus such as the pressure, location, size and length of touch used. Choose a location that can be accessed later on with the same precision. Avoid using clothing as a reference, as it may change.

In the case of self-anchoring, choose a stimulus that's comfortable for you but unique enough. An example for self-anchoring is squeezing the earlobe or joining the thumb and little finger, as we've seen.

2. Intensity

The anchor should be set during the highest intensity of a state. Anchors are dependent on the state. Hence, when a person is experiencing an intense state, the anchoring function is enhanced as well, and it becomes easy to re-fire a similar intensity of the state when the anchored stimulus is triggered.

The intensity of a state identifies how vivid, strong, big, clear or emotional the person feels during that state. As an example, clients are asked to remember a resourceful state. When the client accesses this state and becomes completely associated with it, an anchor is dropped.

NLP suggests that the person should be in an *associative* state of the experience rather than the *dissociative* state when placing an anchor, since we don't want to remove all emotions from the experience.

3. Purity

Purity for an anchor means that the anchor shouldn't have any competing experiences. That means that when a person is trying to access a resourceful state, it shouldn't be mixed with any other states, with contradictory thoughts or contaminating emotions. Purity of a state is its distinctness.

The person recalling a state shouldn't be having an internal dialogue conflicting with the state being accessed. You will need to amplify, focus and purify the state being accessed. When a state is at its full intensity, there are no other states present to weaken its intensity.

4. Precision

Precision refers to the exact time when the anchor is set. You need to identify and capture the exact timing for placing an anchor. For example, when a person reaches the maximum intensity of a state, the anchor should be applied. You should release the anchor just before the state starts reducing in intensity, otherwise a lower-intensity state or some other state will be associated with the anchor. Holding an anchor for excessive time might result in contaminating the state, as the person might enter some other, undesirable state. You must use your sensory acuity skills to determine the exact time and duration for applying the anchor.

The process of anchoring can be used to create a certain state within a person. Anchors should also be reinforced to enhance their effectiveness. This can be done by stacking anchors, by putting extra resourceful states over an anchored resourceful state. The anchor becomes stronger and generates a more positive state. Anchors can also be refreshed periodically to reinforce the resourceful state.

Using anchoring to create a new NLP state

What we're going to do is create a brand-new state. The first step is to pick four states that you would like to base the new state on. Perhaps you have a job interview coming up and want to create a killer job interview state. For this I would pick something similar to the following, but it's important that you use whatever states you wish. So for this example, I will use these states: Relaxed, Confident, Focused and Eloquent.

So here goes …

Remember a time when you were really relaxed. Build that state using submodality changes until the state is really powerful, then anchor the state repeatedly on your little finger. You want to create this anchor in such a way that you can fire it along with similar anchors across your other three fingers. Gripping the knuckles between the thumb and index finger of your opposite hand works quite well.

Once you're confident that you have a strong anchor, break the state and then perform the same operation with the second state, only this time creating the new anchor on your second finger.

Continue in this way until all four anchors are set, then test each one. Finally, close your eyes and fire all the anchors together. Notice this new feeling and revel in it for a while.

When you're ready, think of a time in the future when this resource would be useful. Imagine that time, and as you do, fire the anchor. Do this as many times as you wish. Finally visualize your timeline and concentrate on the present moment. Fire the anchor and move your awareness gently off into the future along your timeline, keeping this powerful feeling going with you, allowing the feeling to settle at any points in the future when it may be appropriate to have this feeling.

REMEMBER THIS!!!

Future pacing (as covered in Chapter 14) takes the anchors you have developed into future situations. You're able to see yourself successfully managing a situation with more confidence or completing a task positively. The mental rehearsal allows your mind and body time to practise the skills, to support your success before the event actually occurs.

Using kinaesthetic anchors, or writing information down, also brings the messages into the body's muscles, making the technique more powerful.

Integrating Your Learning

16. Modelling

Modelling is the process of observing and replicating the successful actions and behaviours of others. It's the process of discerning the sequence of **internal representations** (meaningful patterns of information we create and store in our minds; combinations of sights, sounds, sensations, smells and tastes) and **behaviours** that enable someone to accomplish a task.

It's a basic NLP skill. Modelling is the process of capturing the thoughts and actions that distinguish an expert in some field from someone who's merely competent. The information must be described in such a way that it's possible for other people to replicate the relevant elements in order to enhance their own skill level.

 If someone can do it, you can learn it.

An accelerated learning technique

NLP modelling is a powerful process that can accelerate learning of skills and competencies. One of the core activities in NLP is the study of people who are recognized (by their peers) as being excellent in some field of activity. The purpose of this studying is to identify what such people do differently from their colleagues that gives them such outstanding results. This is often referred to as 'the difference that makes the difference'.

When the differences have been identified, they can then be communicated to other people who can learn to perform the same activity with a similar level of skill and excellence. In this regard, we might recall that **context makes meaning**, and the best results are likely to come from modelling as closely as possible to the context in which the results of the modelling will be used.

Having said that, the person *learning* the skill must have the necessary aptitude, *and* be willing to carry out the necessary self-development. In other words, while it's easy enough to study, or model, the activity of a world-class marathon runner, for example, a person who is severely disabled or overweight, or who refuses to take any physical exercise, is unlikely to be able to translate the modelled information into a personal skill.

Modelling is the ability to fully replicate a desirable skill or behaviour of another person into two parts:

1. The full unconscious set of behaviours that perform the skill.
2. The coding of such behaviours into a teachable/learnable format.

Modelling is at the heart of NLP. Without it, NLP wouldn't exist. It has been said that NLP modelling *is* NLP. All the techniques and methodology that most people think of as NLP are actually just tools designed to facilitate the modelling process. Not surprisingly, then, modelling is the most complex aspect of NLP, and the one that's most obviously still evolving.

As we saw earlier, NLP modelling procedures involve finding out about how the brain ('neuro') is operating by analysing language patterns ('linguistic') and non-verbal communication. The results of this analysis are then put into step-by-step strategies or programs ('programming') that may be used to transfer the skill to other people and content areas.

For years, psychologists, anthropologists and others from the human sciences have tried to adequately describe the interactions between individuals and the way we think. NLP used a different tactic: rather than describe through theory and allegory, John Grinder and Richard Bandler systematically created workable models of their exemplars through application and demonstrable results.

Modelling can be extremely useful in many contexts, especially in a work setting. It's a failsafe strategy for disseminating proven skills. For example, if one manager consistently brings in projects on time and within budget, then rather than sending other managers off on some generic course, it may be more effective to model that manager and pass the results on to other members of the management team. Assuming that experts are brought in to do the modelling and course design, this may initially appear to be the more expensive option. But as the relevant knowledge and skills are passed on, and practical results are generated – fewer budget and deadline overruns, leading to more satisfied customers and thus to more repeat business – the cost should be far outweighed by improvements to the bottom line of the balance sheet, and within a reasonably short period of time.

Modelling is not concerned with the truth or with theory. Modelling is concerned with the pragmatic outcome of achievable behaviour, which is the ability to replicate in full the behavioural output of the person modelled into a set of teachable procedures, so that others may learn them. By taking a complex event or series of events and breaking it into small enough chunks, the success can be recreated in some way.

Natural modellers

Children are natural modellers: they exhibit the quality of exuberant curiosity without thought of the consequences or expectations of their learning. They have a talent to learn at phenomenal rates, given the appropriate support.

Given this, a young child has the potential to learn anything.

It has been shown that to learn a language, for instance, the early developmental environment must include people. People serve as a model from which to learn. Given that a child has no way of knowing how to construct a verbal language without people, they will be unable to develop their language skills.

The school system exposes a child to learning by way of **instruction**. This approach is not natural to how a child learns, and inevitably some are successful and others who are equally intelligent are not so successful. It's not that these less successful children cannot learn – rather, the strategies that are used to teach them are flawed. Many children (and adults) find it easier to learn using a trial and error and experience strategy, which is a much more natural approach to learning than being instructed and repeating information.

When adulthood arrives, the person has been trained into using learning methods that may not have been appropriate for their own particular learning style, hence the reason why some people say, 'I'm a bit slow at picking up things', 'I don't remember much', or 'I have a bad memory'.

NLP modelling is a method that re-teaches the person how to learn effectively, essentially going back to how they were learning in their earlier stages of development.

How does it work?

So NLP modelling uses the same process of learning that you used as a child: the learning of a set of skills and techniques without any rationalization or conscious intervention. This allows you, the modeller, to develop the skills, behaviours, motor skills and unconscious processes that the other person has, without trying to interpret what they do.

Children do not learn by rationalization. Similarly, if you were to rationalize and unravel the complex and unconscious processes and strategies that another person has spent years developing, you would spend much longer attempting to understand them.

So the rationalization of NLP modelling is to NOT understand what you are wishing to learn at the level of consciousness, but to engage your **unconscious** resources by mirroring and matching the other person or shadowing what they do.

THINK ABOUT IT As an example, suppose you enjoy squash as a sport and wish to increase your level of play (specifically your backhand). You know someone whose game is much better than yours and have noticed that they return the ball with their backhand exceptionally well.

By using NLP modelling, you can learn how they do what they do and so be able to have the same performance as that person, minus the differences in your own physiological make-up.

NLP modelling is extremely useful for learning another person's ability that may have taken many years to develop, and to learn it with the same efficacy and performance that the person you are modelling has achieved.

NLP has developed techniques and distinctions with which to identify and describe patterns of people's verbal and non-verbal behaviour. While most NLP analysis is done by actually watching and listening to the role model in action, much valuable information can be gleaned from written records as well.

The objective of the NLP modelling process is not to end up with the one 'right' or 'true' description of a particular person's thinking process, but rather to make an **instrumental map** that allows us to apply the strategies that we have modelled in some useful way. An instrumental map is one that allows us to act more effectively. The 'accuracy' or 'reality' of the map is less important than its **usefulness**. Thus, the instrumental application of the behaviours or cognitive strategies modelled from a particular individual or group of individuals involves putting them into structures that allow us to use them for some practical purpose. This purpose may be similar to or different from that for which the model initially used them.

For instance, some common applications of modelling include:

1. Understanding something better by developing more 'meta-cognition' about the processes that underlie it – in order to be able to teach it, for example, or use it as a type of 'benchmarking'. Meta-cognition is knowing about knowing: having a skill, and the knowledge about it to explain how you do it.

2. Repeating or refining a performance (such as in a sport or a managerial situation) by specifying the steps followed by expert performers or during optimal examples of the activity. This is the essence of the 'business process re-engineering' movement in organizations.

3. Achieving a specific result (such as effective spelling or the treatment of phobias or allergies). Rather than modelling a single individual, this is often accomplished by developing techniques based on modelling a number of different successful examples or cases.

4. Extracting and/or formalizing a process in order to apply it to a different content or context. For example, an effective strategy for managing a sports team may be applied to managing a business, and vice versa. In a way, the development of the scientific method has come from this type of process, where strategies of observation and analysis that were developed for one

area of study (such as physics) have been applied to other areas (such as biology).

5. Deriving an inspiration for something that's loosely based on the actual process of the model. A good example of this is Sir Arthur Conan Doyle's portrayal of Sherlock Holmes, which was based on the diagnostic methods of his medical school professor, Joseph Bell.

Types of modelling

There are two types of modelling used in NLP: **observational** modelling and **adoptive** modelling. Actually, the first type of modelling is more accurately described as a category, since there are two types of observational modelling.

Observational modelling

What I mean by 'observational modelling' is creating a model of another person by copying them in some way. The two types of observational modelling are:

1. Additive modelling

This is probably what most people in NLP think of in connection with modelling. It basically involves:

a) Deciding on a skill you would like to have;
b) Finding a model – someone who already has the skill you want;
c) Identifying the factors that appear to support that skill in your model;

d) [optional] Capturing, or codifying, those factors in such a form that they can be passed on to other people who wish to share that skill.

2. Subtractive modelling

When Richard Bandler first started to replicate the work of Gestalt therapist Fritz Perls, he did so in a very complete way. Not only did he use Perls' particular approach to therapy, he reproduced Perls' heavily Germanic accent, his smoking habits and everything else that he'd heard and seen on the tapes he was transcribing. It was as though Bandler was matching Perls' skill as a therapist – and achieving comparable results – by becoming Perls.

But was this kind of total immersion actually necessary? Do we need to become a virtual clone of the person we're modelling in order to take on a particular skill? In a nutshell, no we don't, as Bandler and Grinder discovered when they formalized their process of subtractive modelling.

In this approach, the modeller will:

1. Initially take on aspects of the subject's behaviour – actions, attitudes, etc. – which they can observe and/or elicit, making no judgements or evaluations as to the relevance or usefulness of any particular feature.

2. Test whether they can now achieve results similar to those obtained by the subject. If they can, then they move on to Step 3; otherwise they return to Step 1.

3. Identify all of the individual features of the subject that the modeller thinks they have adopted. A list of these features will be drawn up – still without making any judgements about the comparative value of each feature.

4. Start to carry out whatever relevant activities the subject performs (selling a car, running a marathon, being successful in a job interview, etc.). On each occasion, however, the modeller will discard one of their listed features and note what difference this makes to their results. If there doesn't seem to be any significant difference, or if there's a change because results improve, that feature stays discarded. If the results are noticeably poorer, then the feature is reinstated.

5. Repeat Step 4 until all definable features have been tested (giving due consideration to the fact that some features may be 'interactive', such as voice tone and a particular form of wording, so that neither has much effect on its own, but they become very powerful when used in combination).

6. Whatever is left after completing Step 5 should be the minimum set of features needed to gain the required results.

The techniques that became the **applications of NLP** were mainly developed by Bandler and Grinder using this subtractive style of modelling. It should be clear, from the description above, that this is a fairly complex technique and not one that's suitable for use where a 'quick fix' or 'cheap and dirty' solution is required. By the same token, however, when the process is used efficiently it should produce far more useful, and cost-effective, results than a less rigorous approach would deliver.

Adoptive modelling

Once a skill or ability has been modelled in the observational sense, it must then be described in such a way that it can be taught to other people who don't have that skill, or who do have it, but to a lesser extent. In other words, it must be presented in such a way that people can integrate the model into their own behaviour patterns. This obviously calls for quite a lot of information, but it must be a sufficient amount of the *right* information. On this basis, it often helps if the people who will be adopting the model understand some of the subtleties of producing a viable model.

For example:

- One of the identifying characteristics of a true 'expert' is that they exercise their expertise unconsciously – without having to think about it. As a consequence …

- Asking an expert to identify their key skills and techniques is usually a waste of time, because ...

- Most experts worth modelling either don't know what they do that makes them 'expert' or they identify the wrong elements of their behaviour as being the basis of their success.

- So, an inflexible, legalistic use of a model – simply *consciously* mimicking an expert's behaviour – may not produce much in the way of results. The model must be integrated at the *unconscious* level so that the behaviour becomes as natural as the model user's own behaviour.

- Effective modelling must take account of three aspects of the subject being modelled:
  a) **behaviour:** what the expert does;
  b) **beliefs:** the 'mental maps' that are the foundation for this behaviour;
  c) **values:** the criteria by which the expert decides on any particular course of action.

- In addition to whatever specific behaviour you wish to model, it's often useful to model an expert's posture, breathing and vocal characteristics when they're in 'expert mode'. Do they sit or stand? Do they breathe from their chest or from their stomach (diaphragm)? Do they speak quickly or slowly? And so on.

The three phases of modelling

1. Observing the model

This involves fully imagining yourself in someone else's reality by using what NLP calls a **second position shift**. The focus is on 'what' the person does (behaviour and physiology), 'how' they do it (internal thinking strategies) and 'why' they do it (supporting beliefs and assumptions). We obtain the 'what' from direct observation. The 'how' and 'why' is gained by asking quality questions.

2. Finding the difference that makes the difference

Traditional learning adds pieces of a skill one bit at a time until we have them all. The drawback to this method is that we don't know what's essential. By contrast, modelling, which is the basis of accelerated learning, gets all the elements and then subtracts them systematically to find what is absolutely necessary.

The important questions are:

- What are the behavioural patterns of the successful person?
- How do they achieve their results?
- What did they do that is different from a person who's not successful?
- What is the difference that makes the difference?

When you have all the pieces, you can refine and sequence the model.

3. Designing a method to teach the skill

Until you have all the relevant pieces of a skill and the necessary sequence, you can't teach it effectively. We currently teach many skills with extra background information muddying the waters. Rehearsal of the natural sequence of the skill is important. If you tried to make a cake by putting it in the oven before mixing the ingredients together, it would be yucky. Yet we think we can teach separate elements of skills out of sequence and out of context, and succeed.

 Find someone who has a skill or a competency that you would like to model, and follow these steps:

Remember, NLP is about modelling the best – so set your sights high: you'll be surprised who'll see you if you come over as genuinely interested. And there are lots of others to see if they don't.

Begin by asking them how they do the thing you would like to do. Identify each step by asking either, 'What happens before that?' or 'What happens after that?'

Remember, many people will not be aware of their strategies, so use your observation to notice changes in posture and breathing to help identify internal processing.

If possible, use a recording device and preferably arrange to see people in a quiet place – I have some very interesting recordings in bars and clubs, but the background noise blanks out the content! And remember to listen – sometimes questions that don't seem very important to you get the best answers.

Remember also that you've chosen someone because they're good – so let them know, and keep any confidences that are important to them.

Mix and match the following question sets:

Introduction
- You have a reputation for being good at ... networking [adapt this to your topic]. Are you happy that I ask you some questions about it?

Environment
- Where and when do you do it?

Behaviours
- What specifically do you do?
- If you were going to teach me to do it, what would you ask me to do?

Capabilities
- What skills do you have that enable you to do this?
- How did you learn how to do this?

Beliefs
- What do you believe about yourself when you do this?
- What do you believe about the person you're doing this to?

Identity
- Do you have a personal mission or vision when you're doing this?

Other questions
- How do you know that you're good at this?
- What emotional and physical state are you in when you do this?
- What happened for you to be good at this?
- What are you trying to achieve when you do this?
- Who else do you recommend I talk to about this?

In short, effective modelling is a very precise and accurate way of carrying out the advice in the old Native American proverb: 'To really know someone you must first walk a mile in their moccasins.' Simply putting the moccasins on is not enough. You must also do the walking.

Having said that, it's also important to remember that the purpose of modelling is to enable people to duplicate successful behaviour. This process is intended to assist in the transfer of skills, *not* to create clones of the expert.

REMEMBER THIS!!!

NLP modelling involves transferring what an expert *thinks* they know and what they *unconsciously* know. It involves being able to produce the outcome and transferring the behaviour to others.

But the use of modelling in NLP doesn't just involve extraordinary skills. For example, you could model how someone keeps her desk clean. We can use the same key questions to find out how someone keeps himself depressed, or becomes frustrated.

17. Change

There are four stages to learning a new skill such as NLP:

Unconscious incompetence
Learning a new skill for the first time, not knowing what you don't know.

Conscious incompetence
Realizing what you don't know and what you still need to learn.

Conscious competence
Building the new skill and capabilities, and feeling more familiar with them.

Unconscious competence
Expertly using the tools as if they were second nature, like driving a car.

Oh, how I'd like to change some of the people I work with at times. If only they thought more like me! Now that you've got all these wonderful insights and methods from NLP for changing people, wouldn't it be great to start to sort out some of your friends, colleagues or family members? Sorry, but it doesn't work like that.

The person to work on is **yourself**. Only you can change you. The incredible thing is that once you begin to do things differently, others will adapt and change their responses to you. So once you build rapport with that grumpy colleague and talk to him using his language patterns, not your own, hey presto! He's compelled to respond to you differently, and funnily enough, that was what you wanted.

Some of you may be reading this book with the intention of better supporting others and using NLP as a tool to coach and train others. That's a wonderful thing to do, and really beneficial to those you do it with, and to yourself. But remember you're not changing them. You give feedback, you coach, and you support, but all the change comes from within.

 Change yourself, not others.

Learn to change content with NLP

We're going to begin with something so obvious that once you get it, you'll be shocked at how many people don't seem to be in control of it.

CASE STUDY

I have a friend who used to have a phobia of worms – not a very common phobia, and one that doesn't really make much sense.

I can't remember anyone being attacked by a worm; I can't remember reading stories in the newspapers about deaths caused by worms, and I've personally never had an unfortunate experience with a worm, but well – she was afraid of worms.

So when I managed to pick myself up off the floor and stop laughing, I had to ask her what it was that made her scared of worms.

This is what she told me:

'Whenever I'm gardening, if I put a trowel in the ground and begin to pull it back, I visualize in my mind, a worm coming up with the trowel. It's a really big fat worm, much larger than a usual worm, more like a fair-sized snake. I can see the slime all over it. Then as I lift the trowel up, the worm is flicked upwards, really quickly, and comes flying up towards my face, covering me in slime. Sometimes it even ends up in my mouth.'

Yuck. Now I understand why she doesn't like worms!

So even though this actual event never happened to her, and was 'all in the mind', the idea of it was so horrible that unconsciously she believed this was going to happen if she dug the garden.

One of the keys here is that your brain isn't quite as clever as you think it is. In fact, your brain can't really tell the difference between what happens on the outside and what happens on the inside.

My friend's brain reacted to the idea of a worm flying into her face in exactly the same way it would have reacted if it was a common event and was really likely to happen when she dug the garden.

But don't worry, because there's one important difference between the inside and the outside. **You can change the things on the inside.**

What if instead of visualizing a worm flying into her mouth every time she picked up a trowel, my friend saw a worm emerge from the earth, smile at her, thank her for helping him to the surface, and then crawl off on his way?

Would she still be scared? And would that image be any less valid than the image of the worm flying through the air?

Definitely not – on both counts, though if she makes the image too cute she may start gardening just for the sake of digging up worms!

Now before we turn this into a technique, we need to cover a couple of simple NLP elements.

Firstly, whenever you remember a memory, you remember the event using representations of your senses (well, what else is there?).

You remember what you **saw**, what you **heard**, what you **felt** (internally and externally), what you **smelt**, and what you **tasted**. As we saw earlier, these are referred to in NLP-speak as **modalities**, and the three we're interested in are the visual, auditory, and kinaesthetic (feeling/body sensations) modalities.

Also, whenever you remember a memory, you're only remembering a *representation* of the memory. You're not remembering what actually happened. You're remembering what you remember happening, but through the filters of your beliefs.

In a sense you're remembering what happened in a manner that allows you not to have to question what you think about yourself.

 Imagine someone who makes you feel uncomfortable, or someone who makes you feel small and insignificant, or someone you have trouble dealing with, or someone who you find difficult to communicate with, or someone who always seems to hold the upper hand and restricts the ways in which you can respond.

Now think about dealing with them at some point in the future.

Right, now in your mind you're probably making a picture of that person.

So what kind of image do you make?

Think for a moment. If this image was real, what element of it would make you feel uncomfortable?

If the person in the image is much larger than you, then that would be scary, for instance.

179

If they're very loud, that would be scary.

If they have a nasty facial expression, then that would be scary too.

What if a boxer, before a fight, imagined himself fighting his opponent, but imagined the opponent being twelve feet tall? I guess his confidence wouldn't be very strong and his chance of winning the fight quite slim.

Usually there's something unrealistic in the image you make – something that in real life would be scary.

There are a number of ways to change the way this representation makes us feel, and for now we're going to concentrate on the **content** of the memory.

So, as a first step, think about some time when you're going to be dealing with that person who bothers you. Notice what's unrealistic about the picture, and make it **realistic**. For example, if you imagine them as being unreasonably tall, shrink them down.

One by one, change all the unrealistic elements in the image to make the picture more normal.

And for step two, we're going to take it a little further, and make some things **unrealistic**.

Concentrate on their face for a moment, and give them a big red clown's nose. How does that make the person seem? How about adding a clown's suit and hat? How about giving them really big flat shoes? Do they seem quite so difficult now?

So what's happening?

It's simple really.

If you see someone with a clown's nose, you tend to not take them very seriously, and this is exactly what you did in your head. This is a perfect example of a generalization. We generalize that a clown's nose always implies someone not to be taken seriously.

For anyone whose parents were killed in a freak accident involving clowns, then please accept my condolences, and find another character you can choose not to take seriously. Cartoon characters, minor celebrities, and WWE wrestlers are good examples.

Many readers may have come across similar ideas before, such as the exercise that nervous speakers use where they imagine the audience naked to make it easier to give a presentation. Changing the content visually like this, especially in humorous ways, can make a massive difference to the state of mind a memory creates.

This technique also works in all other modalities: auditory (hearing), kinaesthetic (feeling), gustatory (tasting), olfactory (smelling). So let's try the same exercise using the auditory modality.

 Go through the people who bother you, until you find one who you remember as having a really uncomfortable voice – a voice that makes you cringe, an overpowering voice, or one that sounds like a dental drill.

So what happens if you change their voice?

If you remember someone who has a deep and authoritative voice, what happens when you imagine them giving you a hard time while sounding like Donald Duck?

Just try speeding their voice up and raising it to a squeak, so it sounds like someone who has inhaled some helium. Then imagine it's been recorded on video and you're playing it in fast forward mode.

If there's someone who tires you out because their voice just seems to bash away at you relentlessly, then try slowing them right down and deepening them until they sound like Barry White. This also works with your own inner voice, as we saw earlier.

Think of other ways you can change someone's voice, and try them out to see which changes affect you the most.

So now you can put all these techniques together:

- Remember five people who you have trouble dealing with
- Think about the next time you're likely to have to deal with them
- Using visual and auditory hallucinations, make them easier to deal with.

Just to give you a start, here are some ideas of changes that may make people easier to deal with:

Visual changes

1. Clown nose, clown clothes, clown shoes
2. Dress them like Shirley Temple
3. Make them wobbly
4. Change their hair – badly
5. Man in a dress – if you're British, think *Little Britain*
6. Big flat feet
7. How about a big perm?
8. Handlebar moustache – great, especially on women

Auditory changes

1. Make them sound like Donald Duck
2. One word – helium
3. Add a soundtrack to the memory: the Benny Hill music is always good, and so is 'Always Look on the Bright Side of Life'
4. Give them a stutter or make them hesitant

So far we've dealt with changing the content via changing the visual and auditory elements. Can we perform a similar exercise in the kinaesthetic modality?

Remember someone who has bothered you, and imagine them standing before you.

Now, rather than changing details about your opponent, you're going to change your own kinaesthetic.

As you see your opponent through your own eyes, imagine yourself getting taller and taller.

What would it feel like if you were the Incredible Hulk and were beginning to stretch your clothes and expand your muscles in all directions?

When you're towering over them, notice them shrink down, then flare your nostrils and snarl at them.

Make them shrink down until they're so small you can step forward and crush them with a thunderous stamp.

Open your mouth and feel the force of your voice flatten them.

Does that feel good?

The more you work with these techniques, the easier they will become. You will also become more aware of what your brain is doing that makes these people so difficult to deal with.

And don't be surprised if you find one specific change that really does it for you. Some people find that changes in one specific modality work best for them.

And does this apply only to people? Of course not!

Try applying the same techniques to other things that make you uncomfortable.

I'm thinking cockroaches in red fishnet stockings and giving presentations in front of an audience who all look like frogs …

Just use your imagination!

Phobias

Many of us have developed irrational fears or phobias that have varying levels of impact on our lives. Whether it's worms like my friend, or heights or snakes, some people can feel tense just talking about them.

Fears and phobias limit our ability to get the most from life. In some cases they can prevent us living even a relatively normal life.

In all cases we can overcome them – not necessarily with 'treatment', but through learning how to manage our own thoughts and feelings.

Fear or phobia?

We feel fearful when we believe we don't have the ability to cope with something. This fear may be grounded in reality, as when we fear being knocked down by a car when trying to cross a busy road. Or the fear may be irrational, as when we fear a tiny harmless spider.

 Many of our fears are a mix of reality and misinterpretation of our ability to cope. When there's a large degree of misinterpretation, it's likely that this is a phobia rather than a fear.

The essential ingredient of a phobia is that it has a significant degree of **irrationality**. The person experiencing the phobic feelings is usually well aware that their fear is irrational, but they're unable to overcome the fear.

What to do about a phobia?

A phobia is an irrational fear driven by our emotions, which is why willpower, facts and reassurance tend to have little impact. Of course, this doesn't stop us trying to intellectually 'understand' it, so we examine the past and try to remember or figure out how the phobia developed in the belief that a rational understanding will reduce its impact (it rarely does, by the way). This search for an explanation is quite natural – especially when we don't know any other way of tackling it.

So, first a few opinions. I've called them that rather than 'facts' because they are, of course, not universally accepted facts. They are accepted by most people in the world of NLP and they are supported by my own experience. Yet many, including those therapists who believe that 'curing' a phobia should be a long and very expensive process, would disagree with them.

1. A phobia is an emotional, fearful response that is rarely based on objective facts or reality.
2. A phobia can happen to anyone – it's not a reflection on one's strength of character, intelligence, willpower, etc.
3. A phobia can develop at any age.
4. A phobia can normally be eradicated in a few hours, at most …

NLP uses visualization to help a person replay an event associated with their particular phobia in such a way as to change how the mind remembers the event.

It's also called the **visual/kinaesthetic dissociation technique**, and it does help the person dissociate, or, as I understand it, step away from the event/fear/phobia and view it in a less frightening way.

To help you understand how we can go about addressing our fears and phobias using NLP, I would like to share with you a case study based on a client of my colleague Naomi Martell. Janice approached Naomi to help her deal with a crippling fear she has had for many years that's preventing her from living a fulfilling life.

Janice has an intense fear of knives. She has no really sharp knives in her kitchen and she doesn't like to look even at a pen knife. She tenses up and looks rapidly away any time there's even a possibility that someone on TV or in a movie may attack with a knife. She hates knives and feels tense even talking about them.

Janice was asked to visualize a scene involving herself and knives that made her extremely anxious and frightened. She had been threatened twice with knives in her life: once by a drug-addict friend she was trying to help and once during a robbery. She chose the robbery. She was asked where on the anxiety scale the scene put her emotions, on a scale from 1 to 10 (10 being the most anxious).

187

She chose 9, but my colleague was aware that she was digging her nails into her hands and her posture was rigid, and suspected it was more likely a 10.

Naomi asked Janice to picture a small, black-and-white television screen with no sound, and place the scene she was visualizing on the screen. Then, she had her move it to a movie screen and imagine she was in the audience watching herself, and then move back to the projection booth and watch herself watching herself in the audience and on the screen. This allowed her to put distance between herself and the event, and diminished it in size and importance in her memory. She felt calmer viewing the scene from each diminishing perspective.

Then Naomi had Janice see herself leaving the projection booth, returning to the audience, and then re-entering the robbery scene at the end. She then told her to quickly replay everything backwards, in about two seconds, as though she was watching a recording in reverse. They did this a couple of times, forward and back. Then Janice was asked to revisualize the scene and see where her anxiety level lay. By this stage it had already dropped to a 6.

Naomi then had Janice visualize a party scene, with children running around and colourful balloons, and knives that she knew were really twisty balloons, even though they still looked like knives. The scene made Janice laugh a little. After that, Naomi asked Janice how anxious she was while viewing the robbery scene, and now it had dropped to a 3. All this had taken only a few minutes, and yet Janice felt so much calmer about the whole knife scenario.

Fast phobia cure

1. Think of the greatest fear in your life.

2. Rate your fear or phobia from 1 to 10, 10 meaning you're terrified, 1 meaning you're not at all bothered (these are known as **subjective units of distress** or SUDs).

3. Walk into an imaginary cinema and have a seat in the centre of the front row (don't forget the popcorn).

4. Float up out of your body and gently settle in a comfortable seat in the balcony so you can watch yourself down below.

5. Put the very beginning of your greatest fear on the screen in the form of a coloured slide. Then run the movie of your greatest fear all the way to the end, as you remain in the balcony watching yourself sitting in the front row seat, watching yourself on the screen.

6. At the end of the movie, freeze the frame into a slide again. Change the picture to black and white and then re-associate fully into the picture on the screen (i.e. walk

into the movie). Run the associated movie backwards at quadruple speed with circus or cartoon music playing, and then freeze-frame the image when you get back to the beginning of the movie.

7. Walk out of the still picture and sit back down in the front row seat of the cinema. Now blank out the entire screen.

8. Focus on the fear or phobia you have been working on and rate your SUDs again. If it's still causing discomfort or fear, repeat steps 3 to 6 as necessary until the issue is no longer bothering you.

---

18. Modality check

Each individual has one primary mode that he or she prefers for learning and communication – either visual, auditory, or kinaesthetic. However, we also have the ability to move from one mode to another, depending on the situation. For example, if you're right-handed, you would probably rather write with the right hand than the left. You have the ability to write with the left hand, but comfort lies with the right.

 Your mind performs six primary representational functions (excluding maintaining internal physical functions such as breathing) in order to 'make sense' of the world.

It **creates representations** of:
- pictures
- sounds
- words.

And it **generates**:
- feelings
- smells
- tastes.

Through the five senses you gather information and store it in a manner that's appropriate to each sense. Your mind then retrieves this information in the same code or format that you stored the experience. If you store information visually, you will retrieve it as a picture. If you hear and store a noise, you will retrieve the information as a sound.

We call this coding or storing of information an **internal representation**. In experimenting with a pleasant experience, you retrieved the visual part of the internal representation of a pleasant experience. Quite possibly your pleasant experience also had sounds. By changing the coding of an experience, you can change your feelings and your internal state. When the internal state changes, behaviour changes.

 Take this quiz if you want to know which sensory system you prefer to use.

Put a check mark next to any statement that describes you; leave it blank if it doesn't fit. There are no correct or incorrect answers – you're simply indicating your preferences.

1.

A._____ I love to listen to music.

B._____ I enjoy art galleries and window shopping.

C._____ I feel compelled to dance to good music.

2.

A._____ I would rather take an oral test than a written test.

B._____ I was good at spelling in school.

C._____ I tend to answer test questions using my 'gut' feelings.

3.

A._____ I've been told I have a great voice.

B._____ My confidence increases when I look good.

C._____ I enjoy being touched.

4.

A._____ I can resolve problems more quickly when I talk out loud.

B._____ I would rather be shown an illustration than have something explained to me.

C._____ I find myself holding or touching things as they are being explained.

5.

A._____ I can usually determine someone's sincerity by the sound of their voice.

B._____ I find myself evaluating others based on their appearance.

C._____ The way others shake hands with me means a lot to me.

6.

A._____ I would rather listen to audio books than read books.

B._____ I like to watch television and go to the movies.

C._____ I like hiking and other outdoor activities.

7.

A._____ I can hear even the slightest noise that my car makes.

B._____ It's important that my car is kept clean, inside and out.

C._____ I like a car that feels good when I drive it.

8.

A._____ Others tell me that I'm easy to talk to.

B._____ I enjoy 'people watching'.

C._____ I tend to touch people when talking.

9.

A._____ I'm aware of what voices sound like on the phone as well as face-to-face.

B._____ I often remember what someone looked like, but not their name.

C._____ I can't remember what people look like.

10.

A._____ I often find myself humming or singing to the radio.

B._____ I enjoy photography.

C._____ I like to make things with my hands.

11.

A._____ I would rather have an idea explained to me than read it.

B._____ I enjoy speakers more if they use visual aids.

C._____ I like to participate in activities rather than watch.

12.

A._____ I'm a good listener.

B._____ It's important that I always look my best.

C._____ I feel positive or negative towards others, sometimes without knowing why.

13.

A._____ I can resolve problems more quickly when I talk out loud.

B.____ I'm good at finding my way using a map.

C.____ I exercise because of the way I feel afterwards.

14.

A.____ I like a house with rooms that allow for quiet areas.

B.____ It's important that my house is clean and tidy.

C.____ I like a house that feels comfortable.

15.

A.____ I like to try to imitate the way people talk.

B.____ I make a list of things I need to do each day.

C.____ I've been told that I'm well coordinated.

TOTAL A _____   TOTAL B _____   TOTAL C _____

The mode A, B, or C that you scored the highest in indicates your preferred NLP system. If A is higher, you're more auditory. If B is higher, you're more visual. If your highest score is in the C category, you're more kinaesthetic.

Knowing your preferred modality for learning and communicating allows you to recognize the way you interact with others, and may also allow you to adjust to a different modality to aid better communication with other individuals (who may have a different style).

19. Applications of NLP

Imagine what it would be like if you could crawl into the hearts and minds of the most successful people in the world today, whether it's the Dalai Lama, Oprah Winfrey, Elon Musk or David Beckham.

Imagine you had the tools to tinker around with their psychologies and take out the programs inside their minds that are responsible for their success: what they believe about life, how they solve problems, and how they relate to people.

Now, imagine taking these magnificent programs and installing them into your own psyche, turbo-charging and kick-starting your own psychology.

Now, with those new powerful programs running your heart and mind, would you do, think and feel differently? And would you create brand-new results because of that?

And if you had to put a price on being able to do that – being able to install the beliefs, attitudes and strategies of the best in the world, internally and externally – what would be the price of being able to do something like that?

You know the answer. Priceless.

This book has been an introduction to the vast subject of NLP. It has allowed you to sample some of its better-known strategies and apply some of its techniques to your own life. There's much more that you can learn and bene-fit from, by continuing to explore NLP and its applications.

As a first step, turn to the 'Further reading' section, which contains many useful books to develop your skills, as well as web addresses to expand your knowledge.

NLP has applications in many different areas:

NLP in business

Basic NLP skills that improve and enhance communication, rapport-building, and goal-setting are all immediately applicable to the business world. Specific skills for dealing with people who perceive the world differently than we do will help improve relations with peers, bosses, customers, and new prospects. In addition, many leaders and consultants in business have turned to the creative and innovative aspects of NLP for inspiration in organizational development, total quality management, team-building, and strategic planning. NLP principles and skills underlie much of what is taught in negotiation seminars. Presentation skills and public speaking are an integral part of corporate life today. NLP self-management techniques, language patterns, and goal-setting are vital to effective speaking. Many of the attendees at NLP training sessions tell us they have come to learn skills that will help them in their professions.

NLP in the caring professions

Much of the initial modelling in NLP focused on how innovative and effective therapists helped their clients change. Most of their behaviour and language was beyond their conscious awareness; thus, the analysis and modelling of the therapists' techniques produced information of a highly practical nature.

The personal change work processes in NLP are unique in their scope and power. They are guided by precise language patterns and a careful, systematic approach for checking the 'ecology' or respectfulness of the change upon other areas in a person's life. Many highly trained therapists are finding NLP to be a richly generative and comprehensive framework for personal change. In addition, the dynamic world of NLP is continually refining existing patterns and adding new developments that help people make the changes they want. If you're in a caring profession NLP can help you with the following:

- Finding tools for building rapport with a variety of clients
- Understanding the structure of beliefs and identity
- Adding zest to your work and increasing your job satisfaction
- Finding new and effective ways to assist your clients to achieve rapid and lasting change.

NLP and creativity

Artists, writers, and performers find NLP training valuable because NLP offers unique insights into what inhibits and what enhances the creative spirit. Applications of NLP strategies provide powerful ways to free and stimulate your creativity.

NLP in education

NLP's practical applications include understanding how we learn and developing strategies for both students and teachers. Through NLP, teachers and parents gain concrete methods for helping children do well in school. Classroom teachers are incorporating key pieces of the NLP approach into their teaching methods and classroom management.

NLP for personal change

Many people come to NLP for relief from limitations. NLP provides freedom from old habits, fears, and limiting beliefs, and gives a structure for new and empowering ways of being in the world. One of the benefits of NLP is more choice: in how you respond, the way you communicate, and how you feel. When you have more options, you can make better decisions. If you haven't been living the life that you want, NLP offers you a path to new and satisfying alternatives.

NLP in health

The applications of NLP are important both to those in the medical field and to individuals interested in good health.

In today's rapidly changing field of healthcare, medical professionals need more than technical abilities. They are increasingly called upon to demonstrate strong interpersonal skills and flexibility, as well as abilities in the areas of negotiation, business management, and conflict resolution. NLP provides these necessary skills for relating effectively and communicating clearly with patients and co-workers.

Medical professionals report that what they learn in NLP training is immediately applicable and valuable in their work.

In addition, leading-edge research in NLP today is focusing on ways of building and maintaining personal health, engaging the body's ability to heal, and defining the relationship between health and beliefs.

IF YOU REMEMBER ONE THING If you always do what you've always done, you'll always get what you've always got. So if what you're doing isn't working, do something different. Do anything else!

Acknowledgements

Everything I am and all that I have achieved I attribute to the never ending belief and support my Father had in me. I am who I am because of you Dad, and I can never repay you for all that you have done for me.

I offer my deep gratitude to my amazing team who covered my duties whilst I was completing this book and all my friends and family who inspire me and believe in me.

I dedicate this book to the two biggest teachers I have had in my life, my animal guides Bhim and Nanook.

Further reading

Books

Introducing NLP: Neuro-Linguistic Programming, by Joseph O'Connor and John Seymour (Thorsons, 2003)

NLP at Work: The Essence of Excellence (People Skills for Professionals), by Sue Knight (Nicholas Brealey, 2009)

NLP Workbook: A practical guide to achieving the results you want, by Joseph O'Connor (Thorsons, 2001)

NLP: The New Technology of Achievement, by Steve Andreas, Charles Faulkner and The NLP Comprehensive Training Team (Nicholas Brealey, 1996)

Change Your Life with NLP: The Powerful Way to Make Your Whole Life Better, by Lindsey Agness (Prentice Hall, 2008)

Richard Bandler's Guide to Trance-formation: Make Your Life Great (book & DVD), by Richard Bandler (Harper Element, 2010)

NLP in 21 Days: A Complete Introduction and Training Programme, by Harry Alder and Beryl Heather (Piatkus, 1999)

NLP: The Essential Guide to Neuro-Linguistic Programming, by Tom Hoobyar, Tom Dotz and Susan Sanders (William Morrow Paperbacks, 2013)

How to Take Charge of Your Life: The User's Guide to NLP, by Richard Bandler, Alessio Roberti and Owen Fitzpatrick (HarperCollins, 2014)

Transformational NLP: A New Psychology, by Carl
    Buchheit Ph.D. and Ellie Schamber Ph.D. (White Cloud
    Press, 2017)

NLP A Changing Perspective, by Dr. Rachel Hott and
    Steven Leeds (CreateSpace Independent Publishing
    Platform, 2014)

*NLP: Maximize Your Potential: Hypnosis, Mind Control,
    Human Behavior and Influencing People*, by Victoria
    Price and James (CreateSpace Independent Publishing
    Platform, 2018)

*The Ultimate Introduction to NLP: How to build a
    successful life*, by Richard Bandler, Roberti and Owen
    Fitzpatrick (HarperCollins, 2013)

Neuro-linguistic Programming For Dummies, by Romilla
    Ready and Kate Burton (For Dummies, 2015)

*Introducing NLP: Psychological Skills for Understanding
    and Influencing People* (Neuro-Linguistic
    Programming), by Joseph O'Conner (Conari Press,
    2011)

NLP at Work: The Essence of Excellence (People Skills
    for Professionals), by Sue Knight (Nicholas Brealey
    Publishing, 2010)

Websites

http://www.mynlpresources.com/
http://www.nlpacademy.co.uk/
http://www.planetnlp.com/

Index

Other titles in
the Practical Guide series

**A Practical Guide to
Building Self-Esteem**

ISBN: 9781785783913
eISBN: 9781848313668

accept,
value and
empower
yourself

A PRACTICAL GUIDE TO
BUILDING SELF-ESTEEM

DAVID BONHAM-CARTER

influence,
impact,
succeed

A PRACTICAL GUIDE TO
NLP FOR WORK

DIANNE LOWTHER

**A Practical Guide to
NLP for Work**

ISBN: 9781785783265
eISBN: 9781848313811